RECIPES FOR YOGURT CHEESE

Joanna White

BRISTOL PUBLISHING ENTERPRISES
San Leandro, California

a nitty gritty® cookbook

Printed in the United States of America.

ISBN 1-55867-158-7

Cover design: Frank J. Paredes
Cover photography: John A. Benson
Food stylist: Merilee Hague Bordin
Illustrator: James Balkovek

CONTENTS

ABOUT YOGURT CHEESE

Yogurt is milk that has been fermented using beneficial bacteria. The result is a tangy, thickened dairy product that is an excellent source of calcium, vitamins and minerals.

Yogurt cheese has a greater portion of the nutrients in yogurt, because the whey has been removed, resulting in a higher concentration of calcium per volume than other dairy products. It is low in calories, sodium, cholesterol and lactose and has a wonderful smooth texture with a flavor somewhere between cream cheese and sour cream. Yogurt cheese can be used plain as a spread to replace butter, or used as an ingredient in dressings, toppings, dips or spreads. It can also be used as a substitute for cream cheese, sour cream, ricotta cheese, whipped cream and even mayonnaise. Yogurt cheese allows you to put foods back into your life that may have been eliminated from your diet, like desserts and dips —and with the added benefits of better nutrition and digestion. Many recipes in this book give you alternative ingredients so you can make the choice for a very low-fat recipe or one with more fat, but still much lower in fat than a traditional recipe.

TYPES OF YOGURT DRAINING DEVICES

You can make your own yogurt cheese strainer by lining a sieve or colander with a coffee filter and placing it over a bowl. Better systems that take up less room and prevent odors from permeating the yogurt should be considered, however. Yogurt strainers are usually available in specialty kitchen shops, health food stores and sometimes large department stores with kitchen departments. The devices are not very expensive and make a good investment for your personal health.

One of the first ways yogurt cheese was made was either to place the yogurt in a sieve lined with several layers of cheesecloth, set over a bowl to catch the whey, or to tie the cheesecloth into a ball and hang it over the sink. The cheesecloth method is primitive and quite messy.

New devices allow you to place the yogurt in a strainer and place the strainer over a container to catch the whey. Some are cone-shaped and others are square and come with the whey-catching container and a lid. The latter is easy to work with, cleans easily and provides a tight seal to protect yogurt cheese from refrigerator smells.

Yogurt strainers are usually plastic, and are made with nylon or stainless steel mesh. I highly recommend that you avoid putting the devices in your dishwasher because the heat may melt or warp the container. Simply wash by hand in hot soapy water, rinse and dry after each use to avoid bacterial contamination and to assure a long life for your yogurt strainer.

HOW TO MAKE YOGURT CHEESE

1. Use natural regular, low-fat or nonfat yogurt THAT DOES NOT CONTAIN GELATIN. Gelatin becomes incorporated in the whey and prevents the whey from draining off. Plain or flavored yogurts can be used, but read the label carefully for gelatin. Avoid the extra-creamy yogurt — it has a tendency not to separate very well. (Occasionally some brands that do not contain gelatin will not separate, and this is due to the processing temperature. It may be just that particular batch, but as a rule I would try to avoid that specific brand in the future.)

2. Place yogurt in a draining device over a bowl or the container that comes with the device, cover with plastic wrap or a lid and refrigerate for at least 8 hours or overnight. A large quantity of whey is released in the first 2 hours of draining, but I have found that at least 8 hours (or ideally 18 to 24 hours) is necessary if you want to reach the same consistency of cream cheese or sour cream for substitution purposes.

3. After yogurt has drained, discard whey, cover and refrigerate yogurt cheese until ready to use. Sometimes a little whey will accumulate at the top of the stored yogurt cheese; pour off the excess whey before measuring. Yogurt cheese will usually last up to 2 weeks in a tightly covered container.

4. Generally, 1 cup yogurt yields ½ cup yogurt cheese. A 2-pound container of yogurt will yield approximately 1¾ to 2 cups yogurt cheese and an equal amount of whey. The quantities will vary slightly depending on the brand.

Special Note. I almost always use nonfat, plain yogurt to make yogurt cheese. The natural variety, free of preservatives, stabilizers and artificial coloring agents, is definitely preferred. Throughout the book, whenever yogurt cheese is called for, this is the type of yogurt cheese the recipe was tested with. I favor the nonfat variety to help reduce fat in the recipes and no flavor because it eliminates the chance that the yogurt may not separate properly. Flavorings and sweeteners can always be added to the recipe later.

COOKING WITH YOGURT CHEESE

- As a substitute, use 1 cup yogurt cheese for every 1 cup (or 8 oz.) of cream cheese, sour cream, etc., called for in your recipe.
- Avoid excessive beating of yogurt cheese because it has a tendency to liquefy, ruining the texture. Use a fork, spoon or whisk to gently mix the ingredients together. If the mixture becomes too thin after beating, refrigerate it for about 1 hour to thicken.
- Avoid high temperatures, long cooking times and bringing the mixture to a

boil, because yogurt cheese is sensitive to heat and will break down or curdle. Adding flour or cornstarch (1 tbs. per cup of yogurt cheese used) will help to avoid separation during cooking.

- Before adding yogurt cheese to hot mixtures, stir a small amount of the hot mixture into the yogurt cheese and then add the entire amount to the cooking pot. Generally, when using yogurt cheese as a substitute ingredient, try to add it at the end of the recipe to avoid excessive mixing or cooking.

- Microwaving yogurt cheese is possible, but again avoid high temperatures for long periods of time. Use lower heat settings and rotate the food several times during the cooking process.

- Yogurt cheese freezes very well, especially in desserts like cheesecake. Make sure that you seal the food well, because it can easily absorb freezer odors.

Special Note. Besides reducing fat by substituting yogurt cheese, many of the recipes in this book give you other alternatives to high-fat ingredients. The important thing to remember when using these lower-fat ingredients is that you should just barely blend the ingredients. Over-mixing will produce a rubbery texture.

NUTRITIONAL ANALYSIS

Each recipe has been analyzed for calories, protein, carbohydrates, fat, sodium, and percentage of calories from fat.* This analysis is presented for a single serving or a specified amount (per cookie, per tablespoon). Optional ingredients are not included. When a choice of ingredients is given, the one listed first is used in the analysis. When a range of servings is given, the smallest number is used in the calculation. When salt is added to taste, no sodium measurement is given.

*Recipes are analyzed using **Food Processor II**, E.S.H.A. Research, P.O. Box 13028, Salem, OR 97309.

APPETIZERS

SALMON MOUSSE WITH YOGURT CUCUMBER SAUCE

This favorite appetizer goes a long way. This could also be served as a luncheon dish by chilling it in small individual molds and serving it on lettuce leaves.

MOUSSE
1 pkg. (¼ oz.) unflavored gelatin
½ cup cold water
2 cups fresh or canned salmon, flaked
3 tbs. lemon juice
3 tbs. low-fat mayonnaise or yogurt cheese
¾ tsp. salt
⅛ tsp. cayenne pepper
½ cup very cold nonfat evaporated milk or whipping cream, whipped

In a small saucepan, stir gelatin in cold water and heat over low heat, stirring until dissolved. Cool to room temperature. With a food processor or mixer, beat salmon, lemon juice, mayonnaise or yogurt cheese, salt and cayenne together. Stir in dissolved gelatin. Fold in whipped milk or cream and pour into a 1-quart mold. Chill for several hours before serving. Serve with *Yogurt Cucumber Sauce.*

YOGURT CUCUMBER SAUCE

½ cup chopped seeded cucumber
salt
1 cup nonfat yogurt cheese
2 tsp. chopped fresh chives
¾ tsp. dried dill
salt and pepper to taste

Sprinkle cucumber with salt and drain in a colander or on a towel for 30 minutes to remove excess liquid. With a food processor, briefly process yogurt cheese with cucumber, chives, dill, salt and pepper until just combined. Taste and adjust seasonings.

per 2 tablespoons mousse with 1 tablespoon sauce *64 calories, 6 g protein, 12 g carbo, 4 g fat, NA sodium, 32% calories from fat*

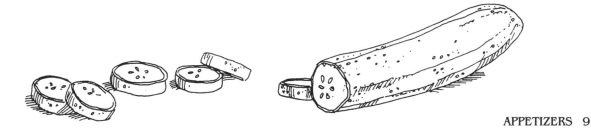

ENDIVE WITH RED PEPPER CREAM

Elegant and healthy — what more could you want! If endive is not available, fill celery sticks or pipe cream on cut vegetables such as cucumber or zucchini slices.

3 heads Belgian endive
1 cup nonfat yogurt cheese
1 jar (4 oz.) roasted red peppers, drained
4 green onions, chopped
2-3 tsp. lemon juice
chopped fresh parsley for garnish, optional

Cut ends from endive heads. Wash and dry leaves. With a food processor or blender, process yogurt cheese, red peppers, green onions and lemon juice until just mixed; do not overbeat. Place filling in a pastry bag with a large star tip. Pipe mixture onto individual leaves. If desired, sprinkle with parsley.

per filled leaf   13 calories, 1 g protein, 2 g carbo, trace fat, 15 mg sodium, 4% calories from fat

CLAM DIP

With nonfat sour cream, this makes a great fat-free recipe. Serve with chips or crackers.

1 cup nonfat yogurt cheese
1 cup nonfat sour cream
1 can (6 oz.) minced clams with juice
1 tbs. Worcestershire sauce
2 tbs. minced onions
dash Tabasco Sauce
1/4 tsp. celery salt
pinch garlic salt
pepper to taste

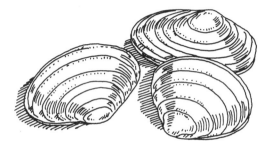

In a bowl, mix all ingredients together. Taste and adjust seasonings. Cover and refrigerate for several hours to allow flavors to develop.

per tablespoon   *14 calories, 6 g protein, 12 g carbo, trace fat, NA sodium, 1% calories from fat*

STUFFED MUSHROOMS

Nonfat yogurt cheese reduces the fat content in this recipe and makes a wonderful creamy filling. A helpful hint with mushrooms is to cut the stem off at the rim instead of pulling it out entirely; this keeps the shape of the mushroom intact and produces a nicer looking appetizer.

3 tbs. minced onion
2 tbs. water
1 pkg. (10 oz.) frozen chopped spinach, thawed and squeezed dry
½ cup nonfat yogurt cheese
¼ cup grated Parmesan cheese
pinch nutmeg
salt and pepper to taste
24 large mushrooms, stems removed

Preheat oven to 350°. In a skillet, cook onion in water until soft and remove pan from heat. Stir spinach, yogurt cheese, Parmesan, nutmeg, salt and pepper into onion. Taste and adjust seasonings. Mound filling in mushrooms and place on a baking dish. Bake for 20 minutes. Serve warm.

per mushroom   *19 calories, 2 g protein, 2.5 g carbo, 0.5 g fat, NA sodium, 19% calories from fat*

CHILI DIP

This is a quick, simple and tasty dip that just takes minutes to fix. Use your favorite brand of canned chili and serve with baked instead of fried corn chips or tortilla chips. Choose a bean-based chili for a vegetarian appetizer. If you prefer a crunchy texture, use chopped green onions instead of green chiles.

1 can (16 oz.) chili with beans and meat
1 cup nonfat yogurt cheese
1 can (4 oz.) diced green chiles, drained
2-3 green onions, chopped, optional

In a saucepan, heat chili, remove from heat and stir in yogurt cheese and green chiles. Sprinkle top with green onions, if desired.

per tablespoon *17 calories, 1 g protein, 2 g carbo, 0.5 g fat, 56 mg sodium, 27% calories from fat*

CREAMY CRAB MOLD

Makes: 6 cups

Unusual ingredients combine to make an appetizer that is surprisingly tasty. You can use a crab- or fish-shaped mold to follow the theme. Serve with crispy, plain crackers or small bread rounds.

1 can (10 oz.) low-fat cream of celery
   soup
1 pkg. ($\frac{1}{4}$ oz.) unflavored gelatin
3 tbs. cold water
1 cup nonfat yogurt cheese
1 cup low-fat mayonnaise

1 cup finely chopped celery
$\frac{1}{2}$ cup finely chopped green onions
$\frac{1}{4}$ cup chopped black olives
2 tbs. chopped pimiento
1$\frac{1}{2}$ cups crabmeat

In a saucepan, heat undiluted soup. Dissolve gelatin in cold water and add to soup. Remove pan from stove and stir in yogurt cheese. Add remaining ingredients, stirring in crabmeat gently. Pour mixture into a greased 6-cup mold and chill until firm. Allow mixture to set at room temperature for 10 minutes before unmolding.

per 2-tablespoons *35 calories, 2 g protein, 20 g carbo, 7 g fat, 175 mg sodium, 42% calories from fat*

MOLDED GUACAMOLE

Instead of a dip, try serving guacamole in a pretty molded form. If you use a ring mold, fill the center with chopped tomatoes or nonfat sour cream.

1 pkg. (1/4 oz.) unflavored gelatin
1/4 cup cold water
1/2 cup chopped onion
1 clove garlic, minced
4 avocados, peeled and seeded
1 cup nonfat yogurt cheese
dash Tabasco Sauce
salt to taste
lemon juice to taste

In a small saucepan, dissolve gelatin in cold water. Heat over low heat and stir until dissolved. Remove pan from heat. With a food processor or blender, process onion and garlic until finely chopped. Add avocado and process until well blended. Add yogurt cheese, Tabasco, salt and lemon juice and process just to mix; do not overbeat. Taste and adjust seasonings. Pour into a small, oiled mold and refrigerate until set.

per tablespoon *24 calories, 1 g protein, 1.5 g carbo, 2 g fat, NA sodium, 66% calories from fat*

WATERCRESS CREAM

A refreshing, simple recipe, this nonfat spread satisfies the sweet tooth. Serve with crisp crackers.

2 cups nonfat yogurt cheese
12 stems watercress, finely chopped
½ cup chutney
4 green onions, finely chopped, for garnish

Blend yogurt cheese and watercress together. Press into a small oiled mold and chill until set. Unmold, pour chutney on top and sprinkle with green onions for garnish.

per tablespoon *13 calories, 1 g protein, 2 g carbo, trace fat, 16 mg sodium, 3% calories from fat*

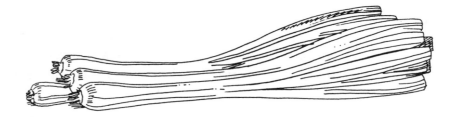

FRENCH ONION DIP OR DRESSING

Makes: 3 cups

Use this as a dip for vegetables and/or chips and as a dressing for green salads.

1½ cups nonfat yogurt cheese
⅓ cup low-fat mayonnaise
1 cup nonfat milk
2 cloves garlic, minced
2 tbs. finely minced onion
2 tsp. sweet sherry
2 tsp. soy sauce
½ tsp. salt

Place all ingredients in a bowl and stir to combine. Taste and adjust seasonings.

per tablespoon *13 calories, 1 g protein, 7 g carbo, 2 g fat, 65 mg sodium, 38% calories from fat*

QUICK BREADS AND YEAST BREADS

YOGURT BANANA BREAD

Makes: 1 loaf, 12 slices

Banana extract really enhances the flavor of any baked banana recipes. Banana extract can be found in most health food or specialty food stores and many grocery stores now carry it.

1 cup sugar
1/4 cup vegetable oil
1/4 cup applesauce
4 egg whites, or 2 eggs
1 cup mashed bananas
1 tsp. banana or vanilla extract

1/2 cup nonfat yogurt cheese
1 1/2 cups flour
1 tsp. baking powder
1 tsp. baking soda
1/2 tsp. salt
1 cup chopped walnuts, optional

Preheat oven to 350°. Line a loaf pan with brown paper and spray paper and sides with nonstick cooking spray; set aside. In a bowl, mix sugar, oil, applesauce, egg whites, bananas and extract together. Stir in yogurt cheese. Mix together flour, baking powder, baking soda and salt. Stir dry ingredients into banana mixture until just barely mixed; do not overbeat. Stir in chopped walnuts, if using. Pour into prepared pan. Bake for 50 to 60 minutes or until a knife inserted in the center comes out clean. Cool for 10 minutes before removing from pan.

per slice *197 calories, 4 g protein, 35 g carbo, 5 g fat, 214 mg sodium, 22% calories from fat*

BOSTON BROWN BREAD

Makes: 1 loaf, 12 slices

This sweet, molasses-flavored bread is best known as an accompaniment to baked beans. Sweeten yogurt cheese with a little molasses and/or honey and serve it as a spread for the bread.

2½ cups whole wheat flour
2 tsp. baking soda
1 tsp. salt
1 cup raisins
1½ cups nonfat yogurt cheese
½ cup buttermilk or nonfat milk
½ cup dark molasses

Preheat oven to 350°. Line the bottom of a loaf pan with brown paper and spray paper and sides with nonstick cooking spray. Mix dry ingredients together and stir in raisins. Mix yogurt cheese, buttermilk and molasses together and gently stir into flour mixture. Spoon batter into prepared pan and bake for about 45 minutes or until a knife inserted in the center comes out clean. Cool for 10 minutes before removing from pan.

per slice   *190 calories, 7.5 g protein, 41 g carbo, 1 g fat, 384 mg sodium, 3% calories from fat*

BRAN MUFFINS

These muffins freeze well. The batter can be kept in the refrigerator for several weeks so you can have freshly baked muffins in the morning. Toasting the walnuts adds a lot more flavor and helps to keep them from getting soggy.

1 cup chopped dates or raisins
1 tbs. baking soda
1 cup boiling water
½ cup applesauce or softened butter
4 egg whites, or 2 eggs
1 cup sugar
2 cups flour
1 cup all-bran cereal
2 cups raisin bran cereal
2 cups nonfat yogurt cheese
1 tsp. cinnamon
½ tsp. salt
1-2 cups coarsely chopped toasted walnuts, optional

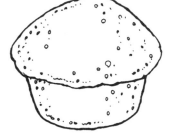

Preheat oven to 375°. Butter muffin cups or spray with nonstick cooking spray. In a large bowl, combine dates, baking soda and water and let stand for 30 minutes. Meanwhile, in a separate bowl, using a spoon, mix applesauce, egg whites and sugar together. Add remaining ingredients, except walnuts. Stir in walnuts, if using, and date mixture, cover and refrigerate until ready to use. Pour into muffin cups and bake for 20 minutes.

NOTE: If using applesauce, make sure that you just barely mix the ingredients; overmixing produces a spongy texture.

per muffin   *62 calories, 2 g protein, 14 g carbo, trace fat, 113 mg sodium, 2% calories from fat*

EAST INDIAN FLATBREAD

This bread is otherwise known as "naan," an East Indian and Pakistan flatbread that is quickly baked in very hot ovens. Serve with creamy-style chutney sauces or spiced yogurt sauces.

4 cups flour
1 tbs. baking powder
2 tsp. sugar
$\frac{1}{4}$ tsp. baking soda
$\frac{1}{2}$ tsp. salt
4 egg whites, or 2 eggs, beaten
$\frac{1}{2}$ cup nonfat yogurt cheese
1 cup nonfat milk, or as needed
1 tbs. melted butter for brushing
spice or herb of choice (salt, pepper, chopped
    cilantro or parsley, seeds, or any herb of choice,
    especially fresh herbs)

In a large bowl, combine flour, baking powder, sugar, baking soda and salt. Stir in egg whites, yogurt cheese and enough milk to make a soft dough. Knead for 5 minutes. Place dough in a greased bowl, cover and let rest for 3 hours.

Divide dough into 12 equal pieces. Roll into rounds about 1/4-inch thick. Brush with melted butter and, if desired, sprinkle with spice or herb of choice. Heat oven to 450°. Place cookie sheet in hot oven to heat. Remove hot cookie sheet from oven, brush with butter, place breads on sheet and bake until slightly firm, about 6 to 8 minutes. Bread will bubble, but avoid browning all over — it is better just barely baked.

per round   *224 calories, 9 g protein, 42 g carbo, 2 g fat, 172 g sodium, 7% calories from fat*

PUMPKIN BREAD

Applesauce can be used in the place of butter or, if desired, use 1/4 cup butter and 1/4 cup applesauce. The nuts are an optional ingredient, but varying the nuts or combining more than one kind, such as walnuts and pecans, will create subtle differences.

1/2 cup applesauce or softened butter
1 cup nonfat yogurt cheese
2 1/2 cups sugar
8 egg whites, or 4 eggs
1 can (16 oz.) pumpkin
3 1/2 cups flour

2 tsp. baking soda
1 tsp. baking powder
1 tsp. salt
1 tsp. cinnamon
1/4 tsp. ground cloves
1 1/4 cups chopped toasted nuts, optional

Preheat oven to 350°. Line the bottom of 2 loaf pans with brown paper and spray paper and sides with nonstick cooking spray. In a bowl, using a spoon, mix applesauce, yogurt cheese and sugar together. Add egg whites and pumpkin and just barely mix. Mix together flour, soda, baking powder, salt, cinnamon and cloves and blend into wet ingredients. Stir in nuts, if using, and pour into prepared pans. Bake for 1 hour and 10 minutes or until a knife inserted in the center comes out clean.

per slice *172 calories, 4 g protein, 38 g carbo, trace fat, 204 mg sodium, 1% calories from fat*

YOGURT CORNBREAD

Servings: 9

Yogurt cheese makes a moist cornbread. Honey-flavored yogurt cheese makes a nice spread.

2 cups cornmeal
½ cup wheat germ or all-purpose flour
1 tsp. salt
1 tsp. baking powder
½ tsp. baking soda
¼ cup brown sugar, packed
4 egg whites, or 2 eggs
2 cups nonfat yogurt cheese

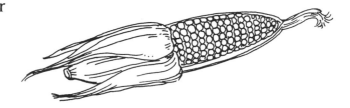

Preheat oven to 425°. Spray an 8-inch square pan with nonstick cooking spray. Mix dry ingredients together in a bowl. In another bowl, stir egg whites into yogurt cheese. Gently stir egg-yogurt cheese mixture into flour mixture. Pour batter into pan and bake for 20 to 25 minutes.

per serving   *182 calories, 11 g protein, 32 g carbo, 2 g fat, 426 mg sodium, 8% calories from fat*

YOGURT BISCUITS

Makes: 15

Yeast and baking powder make this a very light biscuit. This recipe allows you to use more than one kind of flour. Try combinations of flour, such as white flour and whole wheat pastry flour, for a tender treat.

2 tsp. dry yeast
1/4 cup warm water
3 cups white or whole wheat pastry flour
1 tsp. salt
1 1/2 tsp. baking powder

1/2 tsp. baking soda
1 tbs. sugar
2 egg whites, or 1 egg, beaten
1 1/4 cups nonfat yogurt cheese

In a bowl, dissolve yeast in warm water. Add flour, salt, baking powder, baking soda and sugar. Mix egg whites with yogurt cheese and stir into flour mixture with a fork. Knead dough slightly, just until it sticks together. Roll out to 1/2-inch thick and cut into 3-inch rounds. Place on a greased baking sheet and set aside in a draft-free location for 3 hours to allow biscuits to rise. Bake in a 450° oven for 12 minutes or until lightly brown. Serve hot.

per biscuit *120 calories, 6 g protein, 23 g carbo, trace fat, 236 mg sodium, 3% calories from fat*

CORN RYE BREAD

This makes a delicious bread for sandwiches and toast.

¾ cup cornmeal
¾ cup boiling water
1 tbs. dry yeast
¼ cup warm water
1 tsp. sugar or honey
3½ cups white or whole wheat flour
2 cups rye flour

2 tbs. caraway seeds, optional
2½ tsp. salt
1½ cups nonfat yogurt cheese
2 tbs. cider vinegar
¼ cup vegetable oil
½ cup water

Mix cornmeal with boiling water and set aside. Dissolve yeast in warm water and stir in sugar. Mix flours, seeds, if using, and salt together in a bowl with cornmeal mixture. Stir in yeast mixture. Combine yogurt cheese, vinegar and oil and stir into flour mixture. Knead dough together, slowly working in water until a soft dough is formed and dough becomes sticky. Place dough in a greased bowl, cover and let rise until double in bulk. Punch down and let dough rise again for about 1 hour. Divide dough in half and form into 2 round loaves or place in 2 greased loaf pans. Allow to rise until double in bulk. Bake in a 400° oven for 10 minutes, reduce heat to 350° and bake for 50 more minutes. Bread is done if it sounds hollow when thumped.

per slice   *112 calories, 4 g protein, 20 g carbo, 2 g fat, 184 mg sodium, 17% calories from fat*

POTATO BREAD

If you are in a hurry, you can replace the boiled potatoes with leftover mashed potatoes. Use about 1½ cups for this recipe.

½ lb. potatoes
water to cover
1 tbs. dry yeast
¼ cup warm water
1 tsp. honey or sugar
1 cup nonfat yogurt cheese

1¼ cups potato water
2 tbs. sugar or honey
2 tbs. vegetable oil
6 cups whole wheat or white flour
2½ tsp. salt

Peel potatoes, cut into quarters, cover with water and boil until potatoes are tender. Drain, reserving liquid. Dissolve yeast in warm water and stir in 1 tsp. honey. Mash potatoes with yogurt cheese, potato water, sugar and oil. Add dissolved yeast; stir in flour and salt. Turn dough out onto a floured surface and knead for about 15 minutes or until dough is soft and bouncy. Place in a greased bowl, cover and let rise in a warm place until double in bulk. Punch down and allow to rise again for about 1 hour. Form into 2 round loaves or place in greased loaf pans. Allow bread to rise until double in bulk. Dust tops of loaves with flour and slit tops in a tic-tac-toe pattern. Bake in a 350° oven for 50 to 60 minutes. Bread is done if it sounds hollow when thumped.

per slice *104 calories, 4 g protein, 20 g carbo, 1 g fat, 179 mg sodium, 11% calories from fat*

RYE BEER BREAD

Mixing flours creates a great flavor and caraway adds a favorite taste sensation.

1 tbs. dry yeast
$\frac{1}{4}$ cup warm water
1 tbs. sugar
2 cups sifted white flour
$4\frac{1}{2}$ cups rye flour
1 cup whole wheat flour

1 cup nonfat yogurt cheese
$\frac{3}{4}$ cup beer
2 tsp. salt
2-3 tbs. caraway seeds
vegetable oil for brushing

Stir together yeast and warm water until yeast dissolves. Add sugar and set aside until mixture bubbles, about 5 minutes. Stir in $\frac{1}{2}$ cup of the white flour and set aside for 30 minutes to form a *sponge*. Add remaining ingredients, except oil, and stir to form a dough. Turn out onto a lightly floured surface and knead until smooth and elastic, about 5 minutes. If dough appears dry, add a little beer. Place dough in a greased bowl, brush top with oil, cover and let rise until doubled, about $1\frac{1}{2}$ hours. Punch dough down and form into 2 loaves. Place in greased loaf pans, cover and let rise until doubled. Bake in a 400° oven for 10 minutes. Reduce heat to 350° and continue baking until loaves are browned, about 60 to 75 minutes. Loaves should sound hollow when thumped. Remove loaves from pan after 10 minutes and cool on racks.

per slice   107 calories, 4 g protein, 21 g carbo, 1 g fat, 145 mg sodium, 8% calories from fat

BREAKFAST FOODS

YOGURT CHEESE WAFFLES

Makes: 10-12

This is a basic recipe. For variety, add spices like cinnamon and/or nutmeg, or sprinkle with sesame seeds for a crunchy texture and a nutty flavor. Instead of regular maple syrup, try fruit syrups, fruit preserves or my favorite, pureed and sweetened fresh fruit.

2 cups flour
1 tbs. baking powder
1/2 tsp. baking soda
1/2 tsp. salt
1 tbs. sugar
1/4 cup instant nonfat dry milk

1 cup nonfat yogurt cheese
1 cup buttermilk or nonfat milk
1/4 cup butter, melted and cooled, or
    vegetable oil
2 egg whites

Sift flour, baking powder, baking soda, salt, sugar and dry milk together; set aside. Mix yogurt cheese and buttermilk together. Add sifted dry ingredients alternately with cooled butter and stir until batter is smooth. In a separate bowl, beat egg whites until stiff; fold into batter. Cook according to waffle maker instructions.

per waffle *174 calories, 7 g protein, 25 g carbo, 5 g fat, 362 mg sodium, 27% calories from fat*

ALMOND WAFFLES

Other nuts, such as hazelnuts or cashews, could be substituted for the almonds. You can also vary this recipe by using different flours, such as barley, millet and/or amaranth, for a delightful change. These are good served with apple or blueberry sauce.

½ cup almonds
1 cup water
2 cups oats
2 cups whole wheat and/or white flour
1 cup applesauce
3⅔ cups nonfat yogurt cheese

With a blender, process almonds and water until nuts are finely ground and mixture appears milky. In a bowl, mix oats and flour together. Stir in almond mixture and applesauce. Gently stir in yogurt cheese. Cook according to waffle maker instructions.

per waffle   *329 calories, 21 g protein, 56 g carbo, 7 g fat, 161 mg sodium, 17% calories from fat*

RASPBERRY CHEESE BLINTZES

This favorite breakfast recipe can be made ahead of time. Some stores now carry premade crepes if you are in a hurry.

CREPES

1 whole egg and 2 egg whites, or 3 eggs
¾ cup nonfat milk
½ cup water
1 tsp. salt

1 tsp. baking powder
1 cup flour
3 tbs. butter, melted

Process egg, egg whites, milk and water with a food processor or blender for 1 minute. Add remaining ingredients and blend to combine. Sieve through a strainer to remove lumps and aerate batter. Rest batter for 30 minutes before cooking. Into a small, heated crepe pan, pour a small amount of batter and cook over medium heat until holes begin to appear. Turn over and cook for 30 seconds longer. Remove from pan and repeat procedure until all batter is used.

FILLING

1 cup dry low-fat cottage cheese
1 cup low-fat or nonfat ricotta cheese
4 egg whites, or 2 eggs

pinch salt
2-3 tbs. sugar
2 cups nonfat yogurt cheese

Preheat oven to 350°. Spray a 9-x-13-inch baking dish with nonstick cooking spray. Beat cottage cheese, ricotta cheese, egg whites, salt and sugar until well mixed. Stir in yogurt cheese. Fill each crepe with 2 tbs. filling. Fold into quarters and place in baking dish. Bake until puffy, about 15 minutes. Serve with *Sour Cream Topping* and *Raspberry Topping*.

SOUR CREAM TOPPING
1 cup nonfat sour cream
2 tbs. brown sugar, packed
2 tbs. orange juice

In a bowl, stir together sour cream, brown sugar and orange juice until smooth.

RASPBERRY TOPPING
1 pkg. (10 oz.) frozen raspberries
sugar to taste

Process raspberries until smooth, add sugar to taste and sieve to remove seeds.

per blintz with toppings   223 calories, 33 g protein, 70 g carbo, 6 g fat, 470 mg sodium, 11% calories from fat

STUFFED FRENCH TOAST

Servings: 5

Serve this with fruit syrups, fresh sliced sweetened fruit or preserves that have been thinned with juice, such as apricot preserves mixed with orange juice. Vary the extract and/or nuts for new tastes.

1 cup nonfat yogurt cheese
1 tsp. vanilla or almond extract
1/2 cup chopped toasted almonds or walnuts, optional
1 loaf (1 lb.) French bread, uncut
8 egg whites, or 4 eggs
1 cup nonfat evaporated milk or cream
1 tsp. vanilla extract
1/2 tsp. nutmeg

In a bowl, mix together yogurt cheese, extract and nuts, if using, and set aside. Cut bread into ten 1½-inch slices and cut a pocket in the top of each piece. Fill each piece with 1/10 of the filling. Beat egg whites, evaporated milk, vanilla and nutmeg together and dip each filled piece into egg mixture. Cook on a greased or sprayed griddle until golden brown on both sides. Serve immediately or keep warm on a baking sheet in the oven until ready to serve.

per serving *456 calories, 33 g protein, 62 g carbo, 10 g fat, 700 mg sodium, 19% calories from fat*

LEMON YOGURT PANCAKES

Makes: 12

Here's a delicious, fresh alternative to heavy pancakes. These delicate treats are best with fruit syrup, especially blackberry.

8 egg whites, or 4 eggs
2 cups nonfat yogurt cheese
2/3 cup nonfat milk
1/4 cup sugar
1 tbs. grated fresh lemon peel (zest)
1 tbs. lemon juice
1 1/2 cups flour
2 tsp. baking powder
1 tsp. salt
1 tsp. nutmeg

In a bowl, beat egg whites well. Add yogurt cheese, milk, sugar, lemon peel and lemon juice; mix to combine. Mix flour, baking powder, salt and nutmeg together. Stir flour mixture into egg mixture until just barely blended. Pour about 1/3 cup of the batter onto a hot, lightly greased griddle and brown lightly on both sides. These are delicate, so be careful when turning.

per pancake *131 calories, 9 g protein, 23 g carbo, 0.5 g fat, 150 mg sodium, 2% calories from fat*

DIETERS' PANCAKES

This recipe makes a low-fat pancake alternative. Serve it with applesauce instead of syrup for your health. Another alternative is to cut up fresh fruit and sweeten to make a delicious sauce.

4 egg whites, or 2 eggs
1½ cups nonfat yogurt cheese
1 cup all-purpose flour, whole wheat flour or wheat germ
1 tsp. baking soda
¼ tsp. salt
2-3 tbs. butter, melted, or vegetable oil

Place all ingredients in a food processor or blender container and process until just mixed. Add more flour if you prefer a thicker pancake. Spray a griddle with nonstick cooking spray and cook until brown on both sides. Pancakes are very delicate; turn carefully.

per pancake *92 calories, 6 g protein, 12 g carbo, 2 g fat, 194 mg sodium, 20% calories from fat*

QUICK DANISH PASTRY

Since puff pastry can now be purchased in the grocery store, a world of quick pastries are now available. This is only one of the fillings possible. Made with egg whites, each pastry will have about 7 grams of fat. If you use ordinary cream cheese instead of yogurt cheese, it will be far more!

1 cup nonfat yogurt cheese
2 egg whites, or 1 egg, beaten
$1/2$ cup sugar
$1/2$ tsp. vanilla extract
1 pkg. ($17 1/4$ oz.) frozen puff pastry sheets
apricot jam for glaze, optional

Preheat oven to 400°. In a bowl, mix together yogurt cheese, egg whites, sugar and vanilla and set aside. Remove sheets from package of frozen pastry. Allow pastry to warm enough to unfold, about 10 to 15 minutes. Cut each sheet into 9 squares. Place filling in the center of each pastry square. Bring the corners together over the filling and pinch to seal. Set each filled pastry on a baking sheet and bake for 18 to 20 minutes until well browned. Allow to cool enough to handle and, if desired, brush with apricot jam that has been warmed in a saucepan.

per Danish pastry 169 calories, 4 g protein, 23 g carbo, 7 g fat, 114 mg sodium, 38% calories from fat

HARVEST VEGETABLE FRITTATA

Servings: 8-10

Serve this delicious vegetable and cheese combination with a fresh fruit bowl and hearty toast.

olive oil for brushing
2 bunches spinach
2 heads broccoli
½ pkg. (7 oz. pkg.) crisp sesame wafer
　crackers
1 cup nonfat milk
½ lb. mushrooms, sliced

1 large onion, chopped
2-3 cloves garlic, minced
⅓ lb. feta cheese
2 cups nonfat yogurt cheese
1 cup grated Parmesan cheese
3 cups egg substitute, or 12 eggs,
　beaten

Preheat oven to 375°. Brush a 9-x-13-inch baking pan with olive oil. Wash spinach thoroughly; remove and discard stems. Dry leaves well and tear into pieces. Cut broccoli heads into stems, steam until tender-crisp and chop finely. Crush crackers and soak in milk in a large bowl. Spray a skillet with nonstick cooking spray and sauté mushrooms, onion and garlic over low heat until moisture has evaporated. Remove skillet from heat and add feta, yogurt cheese and Parmesan; stir to combine. Mix eggs with all ingredients, pour into pan and bake for 35 minutes.

per serving *399 calories, 30 g protein, 35 g carbo, 16 g fat, 952 mg sodium, 36% calories from fat*

YOGURT BREAKFAST CAKE

This moist cake has a hint of lemon and a pecan cinnamon filling. For more nutrition, use a mixture of white and whole wheat flour.

1 cup applesauce or softened butter
1½ cups sugar
6 egg whites, or 3 eggs
1½ cups nonfat yogurt cheese
1 tbs. grated fresh lemon peel (zest)
3 cups flour
1 tbs. baking powder

1 tsp. baking soda
½ tsp. salt
1½ cups chopped toasted pecans,
  optional
¾ cup brown sugar, packed
1 tbs. cinnamon
confectioners' sugar for garnish

Preheat oven to 350°. Spray a Bundt pan with nonstick cooking spray and coat with flour. In a bowl, mix applesauce and sugar together. Beat in egg whites. Add yogurt cheese and lemon peel and just barely mix. Combine flour, baking power, baking soda and salt together and just barely mix into yogurt mixture. Pour ½ of the batter into prepared pan. In a separate bowl, mix pecans, if using, brown sugar and cinnamon. Pour sugar mixture over batter in Bundt pan and cover with remaining batter. Bake for 45 minutes or until a knife inserted in the center comes out clean. Cool for 10 minutes before removing from pan. Sprinkle with confectioners' sugar.

per serving *375 calories, 10 g protein, 83 g carbo, 0.5 g fat, 367 mg sodium, 1% calories from fat*

CRANBERRY COFFEECAKE

Servings: 9-12

You can make this easy-to-prepare breakfast treat any time of year, but it seems especially good in the winter months.

1 can (16 oz.) whole berry cranberry
  sauce
1 tbs. grated fresh orange peel (zest)
½ cup applesauce or softened butter
1 cup sugar
4 egg whites, or 2 eggs

1 tsp. orange extract
2 cups flour
1 tsp. baking powder
1 tsp. baking soda
½ tsp. salt
1 cup nonfat yogurt cheese

Preheat oven to 350° and spray a 9-inch square pan with nonstick cooking spray. Mix cranberry sauce and orange peel together and spread in prepared pan. With a mixer, beat applesauce or butter and sugar together until fluffy. Add egg whites and orange extract and beat well. Sift together flour, baking powder, baking soda and salt. Add flour mixture to applesauce mixture alternately with yogurt cheese, just barely mixing ingredients together. Spread batter over cranberry mixture. Bake for 45 minutes or until a knife inserted in the center comes out clean. Allow cake to cool for 15 minutes before inverting onto a serving plate.

per serving   *304 calories, 7 g protein, 68 g carbo, 0.5 g fat, 320 mg sodium, 1% calories from fat*

THICK YOGURT SMOOTHY

Yogurt smoothies are generally a thin creamy fruit mixture. But there are times when I want a thicker "shake" and yogurt cheese makes the difference.

2 cups chopped fruit of choice
1 cup crushed ice
1 cup nonfat yogurt cheese
1-2 tbs. honey or sugar, optional
1 tsp. fruit or vanilla extract, optional

With a blender, puree fruit with ice. Add yogurt cheese and blend until just mixed. Taste and sweeten with honey or sugar, if desired. Add a fruit extract if you wish to enhance fruit flavor or vanilla extract to make a richer-tasting smoothy.

per serving *223 calories, 13 g protein, 43 g carbo, 1 g fat, 174 mg sodium, 3% calories from fat*

SALADS AND DRESSINGS

RASPBERRY MOLDED SALAD

Servings: 10

Serve this flavorful salad with heavy meals or as a light dessert. Change the flavor with one of the many bottled juices now available, and a different flavor of gelatin.

2 cups cranberry-raspberry cocktail juice
1 pkg. raspberry gelatin
4 oranges, peeled and cut into small pieces, with juice
2-3 bananas, peeled and cut into small pieces
1 cup drained crushed pineapple (must be canned)
1½ cups nonfat yogurt cheese
½ cup chopped toasted walnuts

In a saucepan, bring juice to a boil. Remove from heat and stir in gelatin until dissolved. Chil mixture in the refrigerator until gelatin becomes the consistency of egg whites. Fold in remaining ingredients until well mixed. Pour into an oiled 2-quart mold. Refrigerate until firm.

per serving *231 calories, 7 g protein, 45 g carbo, 4 g fat, 96 mg sodium, 15% calories from fat*

RIBBON GELATIN SALAD

This salad makes a beautiful presentation. It is especially nice to serve during the Christmas holidays because of the red and green colors.

1 pkg. (6 oz.) lime gelatin
1 pkg. (6 oz.) raspberry gelatin
1 pkg. (3 oz.) lemon gelatin
5 cups boiling water
1 cup miniature marshmallows
3 cups cold water

1 cup nonfat yogurt cheese
1/2 cup nonfat mayonnaise
1 cup nonfat whipped topping or
    whipped cream
1 can (1 lb. 4 1/2 oz.) crushed pineapple,
    drained

Place gelatins in 3 separate bowls. Add 2 cups boiling water to lime gelatin, 2 cups to raspberry gelatin and remaining 1 cup to lemon gelatin. Stir until gelatins dissolve. Stir marshmallows into lemon gelatin and set aside. Add 1 1/2 cups cold water each to lime and raspberry gelatins. Pour lime gelatin into a 9-x-13-inch serving dish and refrigerate until set. Allow raspberry to remain at room temperature. Fold yogurt cheese, mayonnaise, whipped topping and crushed pineapple into lemon gelatin mixture. Chill in refrigerator until it begins to thicken; then spoon over lime gelatin. Chill until lemon gelatin is set. Gently spoon raspberry gelatin on top and chill until set.

per serving 234 calories, 6 g protein, 99 g carbo, 13 g fat, 212 mg sodium, 21% calories from fat

GREEK SALAD

Serve this tangy cucumber salad with pita bread as a salad or as an appetizer. This looks good served in a shallow dish with colorful garnishes like lemon slices, Greek olives and either parsley sprigs or chopped parsley.

¾ lb. English cucumbers
½ tsp. salt
2 cups nonfat yogurt cheese
3 cloves garlic, minced
salt and pepper to taste
1 tsp. chopped mint, optional
3-4 tbs. olive oil
Greek olives, lemon slices and parsley for garnish

Peel and grate cucumbers. Sprinkle salt on grated cucumbers and drain in a colander for 10 minutes. In a glass bowl, mix together yogurt cheese, garlic, salt, pepper, and mint, if using. Whisk in olive oil in a stream until mixture is well combined. Squeeze cucumbers dry in a towel and add to yogurt mixture. Cover and chill for at least 2 hours before serving. Garnish with olives, sliced lemon and parsley.

per serving   *158 calories, 9 g protein, 14 g carbo, 8 g fat, 334 mg sodium, 42% calories from fat*

TROPICAL CHICKEN SALAD

This version of chicken salad has a creamy, sweet and sour taste with a hint of curry. Serve on a bed of lettuce and decorate with Mandarin orange segments.

1 can (14 oz.) nonfat sweetened condensed milk
1 cup nonfat yogurt cheese
1/2 cup lemon juice, or more to taste
1/2 tsp. salt
1/2 tsp. curry powder
1 can (11 oz.) Mandarin orange segments
2 cups cubed cooked chicken
2 cups finely chopped celery
1 cup slivered almonds, toasted

In a bowl, combine condensed milk, yogurt cheese, lemon juice, salt and curry powder with a whisk until blended. Drain juice from Mandarin oranges and whisk it into yogurt mixture. Add chicken and celery and stir to combine. Refrigerate for several hours to meld flavors. Just before serving, stir in toasted almonds.

per serving *481 calories, 28 g protein, 59 g carbo, 15 g fat, 383 mg sodium, 28% calories from fat*

SEAFOOD PASTA SALAD

Serve a creamy, rich seafood salad for lunch. This would be great as part of a trio of salads with a fruit salad and a vegetable salad.

1 cup dry white wine
1½ lb. scallops
2 bay leaves
½ tsp. salt
¼ tsp. pepper
1½ lb. medium shrimp, shelled and deveined
1½ cups nonfat yogurt cheese
2 tbs. minced fresh dill
3 tbs. minced green onions
1½ tsp. minced garlic
2-3 tbs. lemon juice
dash Tabasco Sauce
2 cups low-fat mayonnaise
1½ lb. dry pasta (shells, spirals or broken spaghetti)

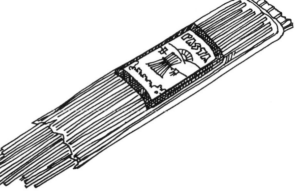

In a saucepan, heat wine to boiling, reduce heat to low and add scallops. Poach scallops until just opaque, remove with a slotted spoon and rinse under cold water. To poaching liquid, add bay leaves, salt and pepper. Add shrimp and cook until shrimp just turns pink; remove from heat and rinse in cold water. Discard poaching liquid. Refrigerate seafood for 2 hours.

In a bowl, combine yogurt cheese with dill, green onions, garlic, lemon juice, Tabasco and mayonnaise. Taste and adjust seasonings. Boil pasta according to package instructions. Rinse pasta in cold water and drain. In a large bowl, combine seafood, dressing and pasta. Chill until ready to serve.

per serving   *433 calories, 32 g protein, 180 g carbo, 53 g fat, 686 mg sodium, 36% calories from fat*

VEGETABLE MEDLEY SALAD

The dressing for this salad has a mustard and tarragon flavor. For a change, substitute ½ cup chopped cilantro for parsley, celery seeds and tarragon to create a totally different taste sensation.

3½ lb. broccoli
3½ lb. cauliflower
4 large carrots
1 pkg. (10 oz.) frozen green peas
¾ cup nonfat yogurt cheese
¾ cup low-fat mayonnaise
¼ cup Dijon mustard
½ cup finely chopped fresh parsley
2 tsp. celery seeds
2 tbs. chopped fresh tarragon
pepper to taste

Bring a large pot of salted water to a boil and prepare a large bowl of ice water. Trim broccoli and cauliflower and separate florets. Boil broccoli for 1 minute, remove with a slotted spoon and drop into ice water. Repeat with cauliflower, but boil for 2 minutes. Peel carrots and slice into rounds. Boil carrots for 2 minutes and drop into ice water. Drop peas into boiling water, remove after 30 seconds and put in ice water. After vegetables have cooled, drain thoroughly and place in a large bowl.

In a separate bowl, combine yogurt cheese, mayonnaise, mustard, parsley, celery seeds, tarragon and pepper. Pour mixture over blanched vegetables and toss to combine. Cover and chill until ready to serve.

per serving   *293 calories, 20 g protein, 143 g carbo, 41 g fat, 639 g sodium, 36% calories from fat*

FROZEN KIWI SALAD

Here is a refreshing salad to accompany a heavy meal, or to serve in the summertime as a luncheon salad. Serve on a bed of lettuce and garnish with colorful fruit.

10 kiwi, peeled
¾ cup nonfat yogurt cheese
1 cup nonfat sour cream
¼ cup low-fat mayonnaise
1 cup confectioners' sugar
½ cup crumbled blue cheese

Puree kiwi with a food processor or blender. Pour pureed fruit into a bowl and stir in remaining ingredients. Pour mixture into oiled individual molds or a 6-cup mold. Freeze. Unmold salad by dipping mold(s) briefly in hot water before inverting onto individual plates or a serving platter.

per serving   *202 calories, 34 g protein, 123 g carbo, 12 g fat, 231 mg sodium, 15% calories from fat*

SHRIMP AND CAULIFLOWER SALAD

This salad is a change from the ordinary, and delightful. It definitely needs the extra garden vegetables served with it for color.

2½ lb. medium shrimp, unpeeled
1 medium head cauliflower
1 cup low-fat mayonnaise
1 cup nonfat yogurt cheese
¼ cup nonfat milk
⅓ cup grainy Dijon mustard

6 tbs. chopped fresh dill
salt and pepper to taste, optional
cucumber slices, shredded carrot,
    chopped tomatoes and/or chopped
    parsley for garnish

In a large pot, cook shrimp in boiling salted water, uncovered, until shrimp turns pink, about 2 minutes. Immediately pour into a colander and rinse with cold water to stop the cooking process; drain well. Cut uncooked cauliflower into small florets and place in a bowl with cooked shrimp. In a separate bowl, combine mayonnaise, yogurt cheese, milk, mustard and dill. Stir mayonnaise mixture with shrimp and cauliflower. Chill and refrigerate for at least 2 hours before serving. Taste, add salt and pepper if desired and adjust other seasonings. Serve with a colorful garnish of sliced or chopped vegetables.

per serving *362 calories, 47 g protein, 148 g carbo, 55 g fat, NA sodium, 39% calories from fat*

PEA SALAD

An old favorite has been reduced in fat and calories by using yogurt cheese. In analyzing this recipe with bacon and with turkey bacon, the turkey bacon added a few more calories, but the percentage of fat calories per serving was 30%.

1 pkg. (32 oz.) frozen peas
1 medium sweet onion, finely chopped
1/4 cup chopped green onions
1/2-1 cup chopped cooked bacon, or turkey bacon
2/3 cup nonfat yogurt cheese
1/3 cup low-fat mayonnaise
1 tbs. dill weed
salt and pepper to taste
1-2 tbs. milk, optional

Rinse peas in cold water until ice crystals dissolve; drain well. Place peas in a bowl with chopped onions. Add bacon. In a separate bowl, combine yogurt cheese, mayonnaise, dill weed, salt and pepper. Thin dressing with a little milk if desired. Stir dressing into peas and onions. Refrigerate for several hours before serving to allow flavors to meld.

per serving   *171 calories, 10 g protein, 53 g carbo, 16 g fat, NA sodium, 36% calories from fat*

AMBROSIA

Toasting the coconut and pecans greatly improves the flavor and adds texture. Decorate with orange slices and maraschino cherries.

1 can (14 oz.) nonfat sweetened condensed milk
1 cup nonfat yogurt cheese
½ cup lime juice
1 tbs. grated fresh lime peel (zest)
1 can (21 oz.) pineapple chunks, drained
1 can (11 oz.) Mandarin orange slices, drained
½ cup miniature marshmallows
½ cup flaked coconut, toasted
½ cup chopped toasted pecans

In a large bowl, combine condensed milk, yogurt cheese, lime juice and lime peel; whisk to combine. Add remaining ingredients and refrigerate for several hours to blend flavors.

per serving *322 calories, 9 g protein, 59 g carbo, 7 g fat, 111 mg sodium, 18% calories from fat*

JICAMA MEDLEY

A colorful mixture of vegetables is served in a creamy dressing with a hint of lime. Serve with a multi-grain roll and fresh sliced fruit.

1½ lb. jicama, peeled
3 medium carrots, peeled
1 red bell pepper, seeded
1 yellow bell pepper, seeded
⅔ cup cilantro leaves, loosely packed
¼ cup lime juice
⅓ cup nonfat yogurt cheese
2 tsp. sugar
salt to taste
1-2 tbs. milk, optional

Slice jicama into small pieces and place in a bowl with sliced carrots. Cut peppers into 1-inch pieces and add to jicama and carrots. Finely chop cilantro and place in a separate bowl with lime juice, yogurt cheese, sugar and salt; stir until combined. If you wish a thinner dressing, add milk to thin. Stir dressing into vegetables and chill for several hours before serving. Taste and adjust seasonings.

per serving *366 calories, 8 g protein, 111 g carbo, 1.5 g fat, NA sodium, 3% calories from fat*

CREAMY CUCUMBERS

This salad or vegetable side dish is popular in the Middle Eastern countries.

2 large cucumbers (prefer English variety)
2 tsp. salt
1 cup nonfat yogurt cheese
2 tbs. vinegar
1/4 tsp. paprika
1 tsp. chopped chives, optional

Peel cucumbers and cut into very thin slices. Place in a bowl and sprinkle with salt. Refrigerate for 2 hours. Rinse thoroughly in cold water and drain well. Mix cucumbers with remaining ingredients. Taste and adjust seasonings. Serve chilled.

per serving *56 calories, 5 g protein, 9 g carbo, trace fat, 770 mg sodium, 4% calories from fat*

RAISIN AND CUCUMBER SALAD

Servings: 6

Always remember when mixing walnuts with a dressing that the sooner you serve it, the better, so the walnuts won't become soft. If you wish to serve this salad several hours later, stir in the walnuts just before serving.

3 large English cucumbers, unpeeled
1 tsp. salt
¾ cup chopped toasted walnuts
2 green onions, chopped
1 cup golden raisins

3 tbs. chopped fresh mint
1 tsp. sugar
1 tbs. white vinegar
¼ tsp. pepper
1 cup nonfat yogurt cheese

Thinly slice cucumbers and mix with salt in a bowl. Refrigerate for at least 30 minutes. Rinse and drain well. Mix together walnuts, green onions and raisins in a separate bowl. Sprinkle mint with sugar and chop into a very fine mince. Add mint, vinegar and pepper to walnut mixture; stir to combine and stir in yogurt cheese and cucumbers. Taste and adjust seasonings. Refrigerate until ready to serve.

per serving   *245 calories, 8 g protein, 36 g carbo, 10 g fat, NA sodium, 33% calories from fat*

ROQUEFORT DRESSING I

Use this favorite dressing on tossed salads and as a vegetable dip.

2 cups low-fat mayonnaise
2 cups nonfat yogurt cheese
2 tsp. garlic salt
2 tsp. celery salt
4-5 tbs. lemon juice
8 oz. Roquefort cheese, crumbled

In a bowl, mix together all ingredients with a spoon — do not use a food processor or blender. Taste and adjust seasonings. Refrigerate for several hours before serving.

per tablespoon   *27 calories, 1 g protein, 21 g carbo, 8 g fat, 169 mg sodium, 47% calories from fat*

ROQUEFORT DRESSING II

This is a tangier version that goes well on vegetable salads, or even as a spread for sandwiches.

8 oz. Roquefort cheese, crumbled
¼ cup balsamic or red wine vinegar
¼ cup Dijon mustard
2 cups nonfat yogurt cheese
¾ cup nonfat evaporated milk, milk or half-and-half
salt and pepper to taste
chopped chives to taste, optional

In a bowl, combine all ingredients together with a spoon or whisk. Taste and adjust seasonings. Refrigerate for several hours to allow flavors to blend.

per tablespoon *24 calories, 2 g protein, 1 g carbo, 1 g fat, NA sodium, 41% calories from fat*

CREAMY BASIL DRESSING

This recipe makes excellent dressing for pasta salads, tossed salads and all types of vegetable salads.

½ cup fresh basil leaves, packed
1 cup chopped fresh parsley
6 green onions, chopped
¼ cup chopped chives
2 cups low-fat mayonnaise
1 cup nonfat yogurt cheese

6 tbs. balsamic vinegar
2 tsp. Worcestershire sauce
1 tsp. dry mustard
¼ tsp. dried tarragon
½ tsp. pepper
2-3 cloves garlic, minced

Place basil, parsley, green onions and chives in a food processor or blender container and process until very finely chopped. Add remaining ingredients and process until smooth. Taste and adjust seasonings. Chill for several hours before serving.

per tablespoon *14 calories, 0.5 g protein, 20 g carbo, 8 g fat, 61 mg sodium, 45% calories from fat*

GREEN GODDESS DRESSING

Makes: 2 cups

Use this as a salad dressing or as a vegetable dip.

3 green onions, chopped
3 tbs. chopped fresh parsley
1 clove garlic, minced
½ cucumber, diced (prefer English variety)
¾ cup nonfat yogurt cheese
1 tsp. Dijon mustard
2 tbs. balsamic or red wine vinegar
1 tbs. soy sauce or tamari
½ tsp. basil
pinch thyme

Place onions, parsley, garlic and cucumber in a food processor or blender container and process until finely chopped. Add remaining ingredients and just barely process until smooth. Taste and adjust seasonings.

per tablespoon *8 calories, 1 g protein, 1 g carbo, trace fat, 43 mg sodium, 4% calories from fat*

CHUTNEY DRESSING

*This is an excellent dressing for chicken salads. If thinned it could be used as a dip for **East Indian Flatbread** (naan), page 24, or pita bread.*

1 cup bottled chutney (prefer mango variety)
1 cup low-fat mayonnaise
½ cup nonfat yogurt cheese
1-2 tbs. milk for thinning
½ cup vegetable or olive oil
6 tbs. white wine vinegar
¼ cup chopped canned green chiles, optional

In a bowl, whisk together all ingredients until smooth. Taste and adjust seasonings. Refrigerate until ready to use.

per tablespoon *39 calories, trace protein, 18 g carbo, 8 g fat, 48 mg sodium, 49% calories from fat*

GINGER WALNUT DRESSING

Makes: 2¼ cups

You'll like this dressing for fruit salads, or use it as a dip for fruit platters. Dollop a spoonful on a bowl of mixed fruit for breakfast or lunch.

¼ cup chopped candied ginger
2 cups nonfat yogurt cheese
1 tbs. honey
½ cup chopped toasted walnuts
milk for thinning, optional

Place ginger in a food processor or blender container and process until finely chopped. Mix all ingredients together. Taste and adjust seasonings. If mixture is too thick, thin with a little milk until you attain desired texture.

per tablespoon   *42 calories, 2 g protein, 6 g carbo, 1 g fat, 24 mg sodium, 25% calories from fat*

MINT YOGURT DRESSING

This is another great dressing for fruit salads or a refreshing summertime salad. This recipe could also be used as a sauce to accompany lamb dishes.

1/4 cup chopped fresh mint
1 tbs. sugar
2 cups nonfat yogurt cheese
1/4 tsp. salt
2-3 tsp. lemon juice

With a food processor or blender, blend mint and sugar together until finely minced. Add remaining ingredients and process until just mixed. Taste and adjust seasonings. Chill until ready to serve.

per tablespoon *18 calories, 2 g protein, 3 g carbo, trace fat, 38 mg sodium, 3% calories from fat*

OLIVE DRESSING

Makes: 2 cups

Use this dressing on meat salads, green salads or as a sandwich spread.

½ cup finely chopped black olives
1 tsp. white vinegar
dash salt
2 cups nonfat yogurt cheese
1 tbs. chopped fresh parsley

Mix together olives, vinegar and salt in a bowl. Fold in yogurt cheese and parsley. Taste and adjust seasonings. Chill until ready to use.

per tablespoon *19 calories, 2 g protein, 2 g carbo, trace fat, NA sodium, 16% calories from fat*

SOUPS AND SIDE DISHES

POTATO LEEK SOUP

This creamy soup makes a great vegetarian meal. For fun, hollow out small round loaves of bread and use them as soup bowls. When you are done, eat the bowl!

10 large russet potatoes
6 large leeks
salted cold water to cover
2 cups nonfat milk
2 tbs. fresh dill weed
salt and pepper to taste
1 cup nonfat yogurt cheese

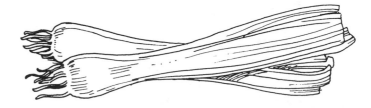

Peel and dice potatoes and place in a large pot. Cut leeks in half lengthwise and wash all grit from between leaves. Cut into small ½-inch pieces, place in pot with potatoes and cover with salted water. Bring water to a boil. Reduce heat and cook for about 30 minutes or until potatoes are tender. Add milk, dill, salt and pepper and cook for 10 minutes. Add yogurt cheese and cook over low heat until heated through. Taste and adjust seasonings; serve immediately.

per serving *375 calories, 12 g protein, 82 g carbo, 1 g fat, NA sodium, 2% calories from fat*

BORSCHT

An old-fashioned beet soup has a new twist with yogurt cheese instead of sour cream. Stir in the yogurt cheese in at the last moment, or serve the soup with a large dollop of yogurt cheese in the center.

1 large onion, chopped
2 stalks celery, chopped
⅓ cup water
4 potatoes, peeled and diced
4 carrots, peeled and diced
4 cups water, vegetable stock or
   chicken stock

4 large beets, peeled and grated
2 tbs. red wine vinegar or lemon juice
salt to taste
1½ cups nonfat yogurt cheese

In a large pot, cook onion and celery in ⅓ cup water until soft. Add potatoes, carrots and 4 cups water or stock. Bring to a boil, reduce heat and simmer for about 15 minutes. Add beets and cook for an additional 15 minutes. Add vinegar and salt. Stir in yogurt cheese just before serving, or serve a dollop of yogurt cheese in the center of the soup.

per serving *254 calories, 11 g protein, 53 g carbo, 0.5 g fat, NA sodium, 2% calories from fat*

CREAM OF BROCCOLI SOUP

Servings: 4-6

This popular soup is here in a nonfat version. Vegetable broth can be substituted for chicken stock if you wish to keep this strictly vegetarian. If you use frozen broccoli, substitute two 10-ounce packages for the fresh broccoli.

4 cups chopped fresh broccoli
1/2 cup chopped onion
2 cloves garlic, minced
3 cups chicken stock
1/2 tsp. dried thyme
salt and pepper to taste
2 cups nonfat yogurt cheese

Place all ingredients, except yogurt cheese, in a large pot and bring to a boil. Reduce heat and simmer for about 15 minutes or until broccoli is tender. Pour mixture, a few cups at a time, into a food processor or blender container and puree until smooth; return to pot. Gently stir in yogurt cheese, taste and adjust seasonings and serve.

per serving *190 calories, 20 g protein, 25 g carbo, 2 g fat, NA sodium, 8% calories from fat*

CREAMY CUCUMBER SOUP

Serve this cold soup on a hot summer day with a hearty bread. I prefer to use the English variety of cucumber because it has less tendency to produce gas.

3 cups chopped peeled cucumbers
1¼ cups water
1 tbs. honey
¼ tsp. dill weed
1 clove garlic
salt and pepper to taste
1 cup nonfat yogurt cheese
chopped green onions for garnish
yogurt cheese for garnish, optional

Place cucumbers, water, honey, dill weed, garlic, salt and pepper in a food processor or blender container and process until well mixed. Add yogurt cheese and just barely blend. Taste and adjust seasonings. Keep chilled until ready to serve. Garnish with a sprinkling of chopped green onions and, if desired, a small spoonful of yogurt cheese.

per serving *110 calories, 8 g protein, 20 g carbo, 0.5 g fat, NA sodium, 4% calories from fat*

GARLIC POTATOES

Servings: 6

Gently cooking the garlic removes the strong flavor and changes the texture, which allows it to be mashed. If you take the time to remove the small green center of the garlic, it will help reduce the "bounce-back" quality that affects some people.

3 heads garlic (about 30 cloves)
2 lb. potatoes
1 cup nonfat milk, heated
1/4-1/2 tsp. Dijon mustard
1/4 tsp. nutmeg
1 1/2 cups nonfat yogurt cheese
1/4 cup butter, melted
salt and pepper to taste

Preheat oven to 350°. Separate garlic heads into cloves and peel. Place garlic in a small baking dish and cover with aluminum foil. Bake for at least 1 hour or until garlic cloves are very soft. Mash with a fork or food processor and set aside. Peel potatoes, cut into small pieces and boil until tender, about 15 minutes. Mash and add hot milk, mustard, nutmeg, yogurt cheese and butter. Add mashed garlic to potatoes; season with salt and pepper.

per serving *332 calories, 12 g protein, 54 g carbo, 8 g fat, NA sodium, 22% calories from fat*

CREAMY POTATO CASSEROLE

Servings: 6

This creamy potato dish is filling and tasty. If you like a little "heat" to your dish, use jalapeño Jack cheese instead of cheddar cheese. Using a reduced calorie cream of chicken soup along with yogurt cheese cuts the fat content down considerably.

9 medium potatoes
1 can (10¾ oz.) low-fat cream of chicken soup
2-4 tbs. butter, melted
2 cups nonfat yogurt cheese
1½ cups shredded nonfat cheddar cheese
⅓ cup chopped green onions
½ cup cooked, crumbled bacon
1 cup crushed cornflakes for garnish

Preheat oven to 350°. In a saucepan, parboil potatoes in water for about 10 to 15 minutes until a sharp knife inserted in the center moves easily but potatoes are not mushy. Remove from heat, rinse with cold water and peel. Grate potatoes and place in a bowl with butter, yogurt cheese, cheddar cheese, green onions and bacon bits, if using. Stir until just mixed and spoon into a greased casserole dish. Cover with crushed cornflakes. Bake for 45 minutes.

per serving *688 calories, 31 g protein, 143 g carbo, 12 g fat, 1393 mg sodium, 13% calories from fat*

TOMATO BROIL

This makes a delicious vegetable accompaniment to any meal.

8 tomatoes
½ cup sherry
1 tsp. dried dill
black pepper to taste
½ cup nonfat yogurt cheese
½ cup shredded nonfat cheddar cheese, packed

Preheat broiler. Halve tomatoes and remove seeds. Place tomatoes in a shallow baking dish and pierce the cut side several times with a fork. Sprinkle tomatoes with sherry, dill and pepper. Broil for 2 to 3 minutes. In a small bowl, mix yogurt cheese and cheddar cheese together. Remove tomatoes from oven, spoon yogurt mixture on each tomato half and return to oven. Broil until bubbly and serve.

per serving   *70 calories, 5 g protein, 15 g carbo, 0.5 g fat, 81 mg sodium, 5% calories from fat*

YOGURT CHILE RICE

If you wish to spice this recipe up, consider using jalapeño Jack cheese instead of Monterey Jack. It's great with plain meat dishes or broiled meats.

3 cups nonfat yogurt cheese
2 cans (7 oz. each) chopped green chiles
¾ lb. low-fat Monterey Jack cheese
3 cups cooked rice
salt and pepper to taste
½ cup grated nonfat cheddar cheese

Preheat oven to 350° and spray a 1½-quart casserole with nonstick cooking spray. In a bowl, mix yogurt cheese, green chiles, salt and pepper together. Cut Jack cheese into thin strips. Place ⅓ of the rice in casserole, pour ½ of the yogurt cheese mixture on top and cover with ½ of the Jack cheese strips. Repeat procedure and end with rice on the top layer. Bake for 25 to 30 minutes. In the last few minutes of baking, sprinkle cheddar cheese on top and allow it to melt before serving.

per serving *277 calories, 22 g protein, 38 g carbo, 7 g fat, NA sodium, 20% calories from fat*

SOUPS AND SIDE DISHES 79

CREAMY PARSNIP PUREE

Servings: 6

Parsnips have a delicious sweet quality that really surprises people. Serve this as an accompaniment to a roasted dinner.

2 lb. parsnips
1 tsp. salt, optional
½-¾ cup nonfat yogurt cheese
1 tbs. butter, melted
1 tsp. sugar
pinch nutmeg
salt and pepper to taste

Peel parsnips and cut into small pieces. Steam until tender or place in a saucepan, just cover with water and add 1 tsp. salt. Bring to a boil, reduce heat and simmer for 20 to 30 minutes or until parsnips are very tender. Drain off any excess liquid. Using a food processor or food mill, puree parsnips and return to saucepan. Beat in yogurt cheese, butter, sugar, nutmeg, salt and pepper. Set pan over another pan of simmering water, cover and cook for 20 to 30 minutes to allow flavors to develop. Taste and adjust seasonings.

per serving *151 calories, 4 g protein, 30 g carbo, 2.5 g fat, NA sodium, 14% calories from fat*

BLACK BEANS AND RICE

Servings: 10

Black beans are becoming much more popular. The rice and bean combination makes the proper balance for a perfect protein.

3 cups cooked rice
½ cup cooked black beans
3 cloves garlic, minced
1 large red onion, chopped
1 can (4 oz.) diced green chiles, drained
1 cup nonfat yogurt cheese
¼ cup nonfat milk
¾ lb. low-fat Monterey Jack cheese, shredded
½ cup shredded nonfat sharp cheddar cheese

Preheat oven to 350°. Spray a 9-x-13-inch baking dish with nonstick cooking spray. In a bowl, combine rice, beans, garlic, onion and chiles. In a separate bowl, combine yogurt cheese, milk and Jack cheese. Place ½ of the rice mixture in baking dish, spread with yogurt cheese mixture and cover with remaining rice mixture. Bake for 20 minutes. Sprinkle with cheddar cheese and continue baking for 10 minutes. Serve hot.

per serving *235 calories, 17 g protein, 32 g carbo, 6 g fat, 22% calories from fat*

ZUCCHINI LASAGNA

Servings: 4

This dish is quick and simple and made without noodles. Serve with a fresh garden salad, your favorite bread and a light dessert.

1 lb. medium zucchini, about 4
1 cup nonfat yogurt cheese
2 medium tomatoes, sliced
½ cup chopped onions
2 tbs. flour
½ tsp. salt
½ tsp. thyme
¾ tsp. basil
½ cup grated Parmesan cheese
1 cup grated nonfat mozzarella or Monterey Jack cheese

Preheat oven to 350°. Slice unpeeled zucchini crosswise into ⅛-inch slices. Place ½ of the zucchini slices in a baking dish sprayed with nonstick cooking spray. Cover with yogurt cheese and top with tomato slices. Mix onion with flour, salt, thyme and basil and sprinkle mixture over tomato slices. Cover with remaining zucchini slices. Sprinkle with Parmesan and grated mozzarella cheese. Bake for 30 minutes.

per serving 214 calories, 24 g protein, 21 g carbo, 4 g fat, 796 mg sodium, 18% calories from fat

YOGURT GREEN BEANS

Servings: 6

Yogurt is flavored with cinnamon and cloves and served over tender cooked beans and onions. This dish is great served with a poultry entrée.

1 lb. green beans
1 large onion, sliced
1/3 cup water
2 cloves garlic, peeled
1/2 tsp. salt
pepper to taste
1 cup nonfat yogurt cheese
1/4 tsp. cinnamon
pinch ground cloves

Clean and trim beans and cut into 2-inch pieces. Steam beans until tender-crisp. Rinse under cold water and set aside. Cook onion with water until soft. Mash garlic with salt and pepper and add to onion with beans; heat thoroughly. Mix yogurt cheese with cinnamon and cloves. Place bean mixture in a serving dish and cover with yogurt cheese mixture.

per serving *77 calories, 6 g protein, 14 g carbo, trace fat, 241 mg sodium, 3% calories from fat*

CREAMY SWISS CHARD

Servings: 4

A great vegetable dish, this one is full of vitamins and nonfat, too. Spinach can be substituted for Swiss chard if desired.

1 bunch Swiss chard, about 1½ lb.
¼ cup chopped shallots
3 tbs. water
1 cup nonfat yogurt cheese
½ tsp. nutmeg or mace
1 tsp. salt
pepper to taste
nonfat milk for thinning, optional

Wash Swiss chard, remove ribs and chop coarsely. In a large saucepan or skillet, cook shallots in water until soft. Stir in yogurt cheese, nutmeg, salt and pepper and heat over low heat. Add milk if you prefer a thinner sauce. Add chard to yogurt mixture and cook until chard is tender, about 3 to 4 minutes. Serve immediately.

per serving *103 calories, 10 g protein, 17 g carbo, 0.5 g fat, 983 mg sodium, 4% calories from fat*

ENTRÉES

LASAGNA

If you want to save time and go vegetarian, use bottled meatless pasta sauce instead of your own meat sauce. Yogurt cheese adds a great creamy layer to this flavorful dish. Refrigerate leftover meat sauce for another use.

MEAT SAUCE

1 onion, chopped
1/4 cup water or beef stock, optional
1 1/2 lb. extra lean ground beef
1/2 lb. lean ground pork
2 lb. beef bones
1/2 cup red wine
3 tbs. chopped fresh parsley
2 bay leaves

2-3 cloves garlic, minced
1 tsp. dried oregano
1 tsp. dried basil
salt and pepper to taste
2 cans (1 lb. 12 oz. each) tomatoes, coarsely chopped
2 cans (8 oz. each) tomato paste

Spray a large heavy pot or nonstick skillet with nonstick cooking spray and sauté onion until softened. If onion begins to stick, add a little water or beef stock to prevent sticking. Add meats and bones and cook until no red remains. Drain off any excess oil.

Add wine and cook over medium heat for 3 minutes. Add remaining ingredients, bring to a low boil, reduce heat and simmer for 3 to 4 hours, stirring frequently. Taste and correct seasonings. Remove bones and discard. Set sauce aside.

CHEESE FILLING

2 cups nonfat yogurt cheese
2 lbs. shredded nonfat mozzarella or
   Monterey Jack cheese
4 egg whites, or 2 eggs

1 tbs. chopped fresh parsley
8 oz. dry lasagna noodles
1 cup grated Parmesan cheese

Preheat oven to 375°. In a bowl, mix yogurt cheese, Jack cheese, egg whites and parsley together. Cook lasagna noodles according to package instructions. Butter a 9-x-13-inch deep-sided baking dish. Layer in the pan in the following fashion; noodles, sauce, noodles, cheese mixture, noodles, sauce. Repeat until pan is full. Sprinkle top with Parmesan cheese. Bake for 1 hour. Rest for 15 minutes before cutting.

per serving   548 calories, 61 g protein, 38 g carbo, 16 g fat, NA sodium, 27% calories from fat

CREAMY MEAT MANICOTTI

Servings: 8

Here's a new twist on the usual meat filling for manicotti. Adding yogurt cheese creates a very tender and flavorful filling. Experiment with different types of pasta sauces and maybe a mixture of ground meats for variety.

1 lb. lean ground beef
1/2 cup chopped onion
1/2 cup nonfat yogurt cheese
1/2 cup grated Parmesan cheese or shredded nonfat mozzarella cheese
4 egg whites, or 2 eggs, beaten
3/4 cup Italian-flavored breadcrumbs
2 tbs. finely chopped fresh parsley
1 tsp. basil
1/2 tsp. oregano
1/2 tsp. salt
pepper to taste
3 cups bottled pasta sauce
1 pkg. (8 oz.) large manicotti pasta, cooked according to package instructions
1 cup shredded nonfat mozzarella or Monterey Jack cheese

In a skillet, brown ground beef with onion; drain off excess fat. Combine cooked meat mixture with yogurt cheese, Parmesan, eggs, breadcrumbs, parsley, basil, oregano, salt and pepper. Taste and adjust seasonings. Pour ½ of the pasta sauce in a 9-x-13-inch baking dish. Place precooked pasta tubes upright in a dish and fill with filling. Place filled pasta in a single layer on top of pasta sauce. Drizzle with remaining pasta sauce. Preheat oven to 375°. Cover dish with foil and bake for 20 to 25 minutes. Uncover dish and sprinkle with mozzarella cheese, return to oven until cheese melts and serve immediately.

per serving   *465 calories, 52 g protein, 46 g carbo, 16 g fat, 763 mg sodium, 27% calories from fat*

CREAMY BEEF TENDERLOIN

Servings: 6

This recipe is similar to beef stroganoff, but with elegant meat. Remember to be careful when adding the yogurt cheese; keep the temperature low and add the yogurt cheese at the last minute so the sauce does not separate.

3-4 lb. beef tenderloin
2 cloves garlic, minced
3 large shallots, minced
1 tbs. flour
1/2 cup chicken or beef stock

1/2 cup dry vermouth
1 tbs. lemon juice
1 tbs. dried tarragon
1/2-3/4 cup nonfat yogurt cheese
salt and pepper to taste

Preheat oven to 450°. Spray a nonstick skillet with nonstick cooking spray and brown beef tenderloin on all sides. Remove beef from skillet and roast for about 15 minutes per pound (or until internal temperature reaches 130°). Place garlic and shallots in skillet and sauté until softened. Sprinkle with flour and stir. Add chicken stock, vermouth, lemon juice and tarragon. Bring mixture to a boil and scrape up browned bits from bottom of pan. Reduce heat to low and stir in yogurt cheese. Add salt and pepper to taste and serve immediately. To serve, slice beef into 1/2- to 3/4-inch slices and overlap in a row on a platter. Spoon sauce down the center of meat and serve remaining sauce in a sauce boat.

per serving   *521 calories, 72 g protein, 8 g carbo, 18 g fat, NA sodium, 34% calories from fat*

DIJON CHICKEN

It's easy to fix this low-fat recipe. Serve it either hot or cold — it's ideal for a picnic. If desired, add more herbs and flavorings to breadcrumbs, such as oregano, basil, garlic and/or onion powder.

8 chicken breast halves
¼ cup Dijon mustard, or more if needed
salt and pepper to taste
1 cup nonfat yogurt cheese
1 cup seasoned breadcrumbs
2-3 tbs. butter, melted

Preheat oven to 375°. Cover a baking sheet with aluminum foil and spray foil with nonstick cooking spray. Remove skin from chicken breasts and coat each breast with mustard. Sprinkle with salt and pepper. Using a knife, carefully coat breasts thickly with yogurt cheese. Roll in seasoned breadcrumbs. Place pieces on baking sheet a few inches apart. Bake for 20 minutes. Remove from oven and drip a little melted butter over each piece. Return to oven for an additional 25 minutes or until golden brown and tender. Drain on paper towels.

per serving *327 calories, 45 g protein, 15 g carbo, 9 g fat, NA sodium, 25% calories from fat*

CHICKEN SOUFFLÉ ROLL

Servings: 6

This takes a little time but the results are worth it. Yogurt cheese makes an especially creamy filling. Serve with a salad and hard rolls for a luncheon.

SOUFFLÉ

¼ cup butter
½ cup flour
2 cups nonfat milk
½ cup grated Parmesan cheese
½ cup grated nonfat cheddar cheese

½ tsp. salt
4 egg yolks, beaten
6 egg whites
4 slices nonfat cheddar or processed cheese

Preheat oven to 325°. Line a 10-x-15-inch jelly roll pan with parchment and spray paper with nonstick cooking spray. In a saucepan, melt butter over medium heat, stir in flour and cook for 2 minutes. Add milk, blend until smooth and cook until thick. Stir in Parmesan, grated cheddar and salt; batter should be thick. Add a small amount of batter to egg yolks, mix well and add back to batter. In a separate bowl, beat egg whites until stiff. Fold egg whites into batter. Pour batter into prepared pan and spread evenly. Bake for 40 minutes until golden brown and soufflé springs back when touched. Prepare filling while baking soufflé.

FILLING

½ cup chopped onion
¼ lb. mushrooms, chopped
2 pkg. (10 oz. each) frozen chopped
   spinach, thawed, squeezed dry
1 cup diced, cooked chicken

2 tsp. Dijon mustard
¾ cup nonfat yogurt cheese
dash nutmeg
salt and pepper to taste

Spray a skillet with nonstick cooking spray and sauté onion and mushrooms over medium-high heat until soft and liquid has evaporated from mushrooms. Add spinach to pan and stir to combine. Add chicken, mustard, yogurt cheese, nutmeg, salt and pepper and stir until just combined. Taste and adjust seasonings. Remove from heat and cool to room temperature.

Preheat broiler. Run a sharp knife around the edges of the soufflé. Place a piece of parchment on top of soufflé and turn it over. Peel off parchment from bottom of soufflé, place another piece of parchment on top and invert again, so the filling will be placed on the browned side of the soufflé. Spread filling over soufflé and roll up lengthwise. Slide onto a greased baking sheet. Cut cheese slices into triangles and place on top of roll for garnish. Broil until cheese is slightly browned.

per serving   *358 calories, 31 g protein, 40 g carbo, 16 g fat, NA sodium, 33% calories from fat*

CHICKEN AND VEGETABLE FETTUCCINE

When using vegetable spray instead of butter for sautéing, always be ready to add a little water or stock to help prevent food from sticking.

2 cups sliced carrots
2 lb. chicken breasts, skinned and boned
1 cup chopped onion
½ tsp. dried basil
3 cloves garlic, minced
salt and pepper to taste

¼ cup chicken stock, optional
4 cups sliced zucchini
1½ cups nonfat yogurt cheese
8 cups cooked fettuccine noodles
¼-½ cup grated Parmesan cheese

Steam or boil carrots until just tender-crisp and set aside. Cut chicken breasts into bite-sized pieces. Spray a nonstick skillet with nonstick cooking spray and sauté chicken over medium-high heat with onion, basil, garlic, salt and pepper until chicken has lost its pink color, about 4 minutes. If chicken sticks, add a little chicken stock. Remove chicken from skillet. In same skillet, sauté zucchini until tender. Add carrots and reheat. Reduce heat and add yogurt cheese. Stir until cheese just begins to melt. Remove from heat, add noodles and chicken and toss to combine. Sprinkle with Parmesan. Taste and adjust seasonings.

per serving *467 calories, 49 g protein, 51 g carbo, 6 g fat, NA sodium, 12% calories from fat*

CHICKEN WITH CHILE STRIPS

Servings: 6

Yogurt cheese makes this Mexican dish creamy and rich-tasting, and it will have them coming back for more. Serve with a rice accompaniment and maybe a broiled tomato or green salad.

6 chicken breast halves, skinned and boned
salt and pepper to taste
1/4 cup chicken stock, optional
1 large onion, sliced

3 cans (7 oz. each) whole green chiles
2/3 cup 2% milk
1/2 -1 tsp. salt
2 cups nonfat yogurt cheese
1/3 lb. grated nonfat cheddar cheese

Preheat oven to 350°. Cut each chicken breast lengthwise into 4 fillets. Season with salt and pepper. Spray a nonstick skillet with nonstick cooking spray and sauté fillets over medium heat until lightly browned; if meat tends to stick, add a little chicken stock. Remove from pan and set aside. Spray skillet again and sauté onion until soft. Set aside 7 of the green chiles and cut remaining chiles into strips. Add strips to skillet cook for 5 minutes. Process remaining 7 chiles with milk in a food processor or blender. Add salt and yogurt cheese and process until just combined; do not over-process. Place 1/2 of the fillets in a baking dish. Cover with 1/2 of the onion-chile mixture, 1/2 of the sauce and 1/2 of the cheese. Repeat. Bake for 30 minutes.

per serving   *376 calories, 58 g protein, 44 g carbo, 6 g fat, NA sodium, 11% calories from fat*

STUFFED CHICKEN

The stuffing is actually stuffed under the skin in order to create a juicy result. Serve this with a creamy rice or potato dish and colorful vegetables.

2 chickens, 3½ lb. each
1½ cups nonfat yogurt cheese
1 tbs. lemon juice
¼ cup finely chopped green onions
¼ cup chopped fresh parsley

4 cloves garlic, minced
salt and pepper to taste
1 tbs. melted butter for brushing
paprika

Preheat oven to 400°. Cut chickens into 2 pieces through the backbone from tail to neck. Trim off any excess fat and discard wing tips. Gently loosen skin by inserting your hand between flesh and skin. (Try to leave the skin on the edges intact). In a bowl, mix together yogurt cheese, lemon juice, green onions, parsley, garlic, salt and pepper. Taste mixture and adjust seasonings. Distribute mixture evenly under the skin of the chickens. Place chickens skin side up in a shallow roasting pan. Brush melted butter over skin and sprinkle with paprika. Bake for 45 minutes to 1 hour or until juices run clear instead of pink. Cut into serving pieces and serve immediately.

per serving   *253 calories, 39 g protein, 8 g carbo, 6 g fat, NA sodium, 24% calories from fat*

DILLED SALMON

Yogurt cheese reduces the fat content of this quick and simple recipe. Serve it hot or cold. If desired, the sauce can be gently warmed and served as an accompaniment instead of baking it over the fish.

½ cup balsamic or red wine vinegar
1 tsp. dried dill weed
½ tsp. black pepper
1 tsp. salt
1 cup nonfat evaporated milk
1 cup nonfat yogurt cheese
12 salmon fillets, 8 oz. each
fresh dill sprigs for garnish

Preheat oven to 350°. Spray a shallow baking dish with nonstick cooking spray. In a small saucepan, mix together vinegar, dill weed, pepper and salt; simmer over medium heat for 5 minutes to reduce. Cool slightly, mix with milk and yogurt cheese and set aside. Place fish fillets in a single layer in baking dish. Bake for 10 minutes. Pour cheese mixture over top and return to oven to bake for an additional 10 to 20 minutes or until fish flakes easily with a fork. Garnish with dill sprigs.

per serving *297 calories, 51 g protein, 4 g carbo, 8 g fat, 362 mg sodium, 24% calories from fat*

PASTA SPINACH ROLL

Pasta is filled and rolled up similar to a jelly roll, tied in cheesecloth and boiled. This beautiful presentation takes a little time but makes an elegant entrée. Serve with your favorite meat sauce or a tomato sauce if you wish a vegetarian dish.

1½ cups flour
2 eggs
1 tbs. vegetable oil
pinch salt
2 pkg. (10 oz. each) frozen chopped spinach, thawed, squeezed dry
1¼ cups nonfat yogurt cheese
½ cup grated Parmesan cheese
4 egg whites, or 2 eggs, beaten
1 tbs. minced onion
1 tbs. flour
½ cup low-fat dry cottage cheese
½ cup shredded low-fat Monterey Jack cheese
½ tsp. nutmeg
salt and pepper to taste
bottled pasta sauce
grated Parmesan cheese

Mix 1½ cups flour, eggs, oil and salt together and knead until smooth. Let pasta dough rest for 15 minutes. In a bowl, mix spinach with yogurt cheese, Parmesan, egg whites, onion, 1 tbs. flour, cottage cheese, Jack cheese, nutmeg, salt and pepper. Taste and adjust seasonings. Roll out pasta dough very thinly into a rectangle and cover with filling to within 1 inch of edge. Roll up jelly roll-fashion from the long side. Roll in a double layer of cheesecloth and tie both ends with a string, keeping ends of string long to help remove from pot later. Cook in simmering salted water for 50 to 60 minutes. Remove pasta from water with string handles, immediately remove cheesecloth and allow to cool for several minutes before cutting into rounds. Serve on a platter accompanied by your favorite pasta sauce and a dish of Parmesan cheese for sprinkling.

per serving without pasta sauce *199 calories, 15 g protein, 22 g carbo, 6 g fat, NA sodium, 25% calories from fat*

SHRIMP AND VEGETABLE SHELLS

Here's a change from the ordinary. Serve several filled shells on a bed of lettuce and, if desired, sprinkle with a little chopped red pepper, chopped red onion and/or parsley.

1 lb. jumbo pasta shells
1 cup nonfat yogurt cheese
2 tbs. low-fat mayonnaise
1 tbs. lemon juice
1-2 tsp. sugar
2 cups cooked baby shrimp

2 cups chopped celery
2 cups grated carrots
½ cup chopped water chestnuts
½ cup chopped green onions
2 cups shredded nonfat cheddar cheese
salt and pepper to taste, optional

Cook pasta shells according to package directions. Mix together yogurt cheese, mayonnaise, lemon juice and sugar. In a bowl, combine shrimp, celery, carrots, water chestnuts, green onions and cheddar cheese. Stir in yogurt cheese mixture. Taste and add salt and pepper if desired. Fill shells with shrimp mixture and serve on a bed of lettuce.

per serving   *306 calories, 25 g protein, 76 g carbo, 5 g fat, NA sodium, 11% calories from fat*

CHEESY HERB QUICHE

Servings: 8

Quiche is good for any meal, even dinner. Serve with a crispy garden salad and crusty bread. If you want a lower-fat alternative to a pastry crust, try the pizza crust dough found in a cylinder in the refrigerator case of your grocery store.

pastry for 11-inch quiche
1 cup nonfat yogurt cheese
2 eggs and 4 egg whites, or 4 eggs
3 tbs. flour
1/2 cup nonfat sour cream
1 cup nonfat milk
1 cup nonfat evaporated milk

salt and pepper to taste
1 cup grated nonfat Swiss cheese
1/4 cup chopped chives
1/2 cup chopped parsley
1/2 cup chopped green onions
1/4 cup grated Parmesan cheese

Preheat oven to 375°. Line an 11-inch quiche pan or dish with pastry. In a bowl, combine yogurt cheese, egg and egg whites, flour, sour cream, milk, evaporated milk, salt and pepper and set aside. Sprinkle Swiss cheese over bottom of pastry. Sprinkle chives, parsley and green onions over cheese. Pour egg mixture over all and sprinkle with Parmesan. Bake for 45 minutes or until custard is set and a knife inserted in the center comes out clean.

per serving *268 calories, 36 g protein, 56 g carbo, 10 g fat, NA sodium, 20% calories from fat*

CREAMY CHEESE MANICOTTI

Servings: 8

When yogurt cheese is substituted for ricotta cheese, the results are a creamier and lighter texture with a slight tang. In a pinch, I made this recipe using stewed tomatoes as the sauce and was pleasantly surprised.

1 pkg. (8 oz.) large manicotti pasta
3 cups nonfat yogurt cheese
2 eggs, beaten, or 4 egg whites
2 cups shredded nonfat mozzarella or
    Monterey Jack cheese
1/2 cup grated Parmesan cheese

2 tbs. chopped fresh parsley
2 tbs. chopped fresh basil, or 2 tsp. dried
1 tsp. oregano
pepper to taste
3 cups bottled pasta sauce

Boil pasta according to package directions, rinse with cold water and drain while preparing filling. Mix together yogurt cheese, egg whites, 1 cup of the mozzarella, Parmesan, parsley, basil, oregano and pepper. Taste and adjust seasonings. Preheat oven to 375°. Pour 1/2 of the pasta sauce in a 9-x-13-inch baking dish. Place each precooked manicotti tube upright in a bowl and fill with filling. Carefully place filled tubes over pasta sauce in a single layer. Pour remaining pasta sauce over filled manicotti. Cover dish with foil and bake for 20 minutes. Uncover, sprinkle with remaining mozzarella and return to oven until cheese melts. Serve immediately.

per serving   *372 calories, 50 g protein, 49 g carbo, 6 g fat, 859 mg sodium, 11% calories from fat*

VEGETARIAN SPINACH AND ARTICHOKE BAKE

Even kids enjoy this vegetable dish. The yogurt makes it especially creamy and artichokes give this recipe texture.

6 pkg. (10 oz. each) frozen chopped
    spinach
4 jars (4 oz. each) marinated artichoke
    hearts
2-4 tbs. vinegar (prefer balsamic)

1 jar (2 oz.) chopped pimientos
2 cups nonfat yogurt cheese
2 tbs. low-fat mayonnaise
1½ cups grated Parmesan cheese

Preheat oven to 350°. Thaw chopped spinach and squeeze dry. Butter a 6- to 8-cup baking dish. Place ½ of the spinach in dish. Drain artichokes, reserving liquid. Cut artichokes into quarters and place ½ of them over spinach. Drizzle a little of the reserved marinade and a little vinegar over spinach.

Sprinkle with ½ of the chopped pimientos. Mix yogurt cheese with mayonnaise and spread ½ of this mixture over everything. Repeat layers and top with grated Parmesan. Bake for 40 minutes.

per serving   272 calories, 22 g protein, 38 g carbo, 15 g fat, 954 mg sodium, 37% calories from fat

EGGPLANT CASSEROLE

In this Italian vegetarian entrée, the ricotta has been replaced with yogurt cheese.

1½ lb. eggplants
olive oil for brushing
salt and pepper to taste
1 medium onion, chopped
2 cloves garlic, minced
1 lb. fresh tomatoes, skinned and seeded
1 tsp. dried basil
½ tsp. dried oregano
pinch sugar
2 tbs. chopped fresh parsley
¼ cup red wine
½ cup nonfat yogurt cheese
2 egg whites, or 1 egg, beaten
⅓ cup grated Parmesan cheese
½ cup nonfat evaporated milk
grated Parmesan for garnish

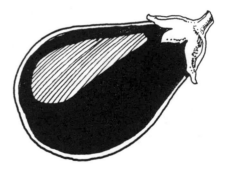

Preheat broiler. Peel eggplants and cut into ¼-inch rounds. Brush both sides with olive oil, sprinkle with salt and pepper and broil 6 inches from heat for about 4 minutes per side, until lightly browned.

Spray a skillet with nonstick cooking spray and sauté onion and garlic until softened; if onion and garlic begin to brown, add a little water. Coarsely chop tomatoes and add to skillet with basil, oregano, sugar, parsley, wine, salt and pepper. Cook briefly at high heat; lower heat and simmer until liquid has cooked away. In a bowl, mix yogurt cheese, egg whites, ⅓ cup Parmesan cheese and evaporated milk together and set aside.

Spray a medium baking dish with nonstick cooking spray. Arrange ½ of the eggplant rounds in dish, cover with tomato mixture, place remaining eggplant rounds on top and pour on cheese mixture. Sprinkle with additional Parmesan. Bake for 10 minutes, reduce heat to 375° and bake for an additional 20 minutes or until top is golden brown and the center is firm to the touch.

per serving *115 calories, 10 g protein, 13 g carbo, 3 g fat, NA sodium, 25% calories from fat*

SPREADS, DIPS AND SAUCES

SAVORY HERB CHEESE

Makes: 1 cup

Experiment with the taste of different herbs. Tarragon is reminiscent of licorice, chervil is very subtle, and dill is well known with a slightly bitter taste. If fresh herbs are not available, use 1 tsp. dried herbs.

1 cup nonfat yogurt cheese
2 tbs. chopped fresh parsley

1 tbs. chopped fresh tarragon, chervil
  or dill

In a bowl, mix together all ingredients. Taste and adjust seasonings.

per tablespoon *16 calories, 2 g protein, 2 g carbo, trace fat, 29 mg sodium, 3% calories from fat*

PARMESAN HERB CHEESE

Makes: 1 cup

You'll like this spread on hot toasted bread rounds or bagels. It can also be served as a dip or a sandwich spread.

½ cup nonfat yogurt cheese
¼ cup chopped fresh parsley
⅓ cup grated Parmesan cheese
1-2 cloves garlic, minced

½ tsp. dried basil
¼ tsp. dried oregano
¼ tsp. salt
¼ tsp. pepper

In a bowl, mix together all ingredients. Taste and adjust seasonings.

per tablespoon *18 calories, 2 g protein, 1 g carbo, 0.5 g fat, 83 mg sodium, 33% calories from fat*

HERB SPREAD FOR VEGETABLES

Makes: 1¼ cups

Fill a piping bag and pipe this spread onto fresh vegetables like cucumbers or celery for a tasty and fat-free appetizer.

1 clove garlic, minced
¼ cup chopped fresh parsley
2 green onions, chopped
dash Tabasco Sauce
1 tbs. white wine
1 cup nonfat yogurt cheese
white pepper to taste

With a food processor or blender, finely mince garlic, parsley and green onions together. Add Tabasco and white wine and process to mix. Add yogurt cheese and white pepper and process until just combined; do not overprocess. Taste and adjust seasonings.

per tablespoon *14 calories, 1 g protein, 2 g carbo, trace fat, 18 mg sodium, 3% calories from fat*

BASIL CHEESE SPREAD

Makes: 1⅓ cups

Use this as a spread for bagels, toasted French bread or crackers. This recipe could also be used as a topping for sliced tomatoes and quickly broiled as a vegetable accompaniment to an entrée.

1 cup nonfat yogurt cheese
¼ cup chopped fresh basil
2 tsp. tomato paste
2 cloves garlic, minced
salt and pepper to taste

With a food processor or mixer, quickly blend all ingredients together. Taste and adjust seasonings.

per tablespoon *13 calories, 1 g protein, 2 g carbo, trace fat, NA sodium, 4% calories from fat*

AVOCADO CHEESE

Makes: 2 cups

The Haas variety of avocado is preferred, because the flavor is better. This makes a subtle green spread that can be used with vegetables or crackers. Garnish with a few strips of pimiento or a sprinkle of finely chopped red peppers.

2 large avocados
1 cup nonfat yogurt cheese

2 tsp. lemon juice
salt to taste, optional

Remove skins and seeds from avocados and blend with a food processor, blender or mixer until smooth. Mix in remaining ingredients and process until just mixed. Taste and adjust seasonings.

per tablespoon *27 calories, 1 g protein, 2 g carbo, 2 g fat, 12 mg sodium, 60% calories from fat*

OLIVE AND NUT SPREAD

Makes: 3 cups

This can be used as a sandwich spread or as a dip for vegetables. For a more pungent flavor, add 2 tbs. capers.

2 cups nonfat yogurt cheese
½ cup chopped stuffed green olives

½ cup chopped toasted walnuts or
   pecans

Mix all ingredients together and refrigerate until ready to serve.

per tablespoon *20 calories, 1 g protein, 2 g carbo, 1 g fat, 54 mg sodium, 43% calories from fat*

BACON AND ONION SPREAD

A thousand possible uses for this spread come to mind. This flavor combination is extremely popular. Serve it with a selection of small bread rounds and slices of tomato to top.

12 slices bacon
2 cups nonfat yogurt cheese
½ cup finely chopped green onion
pepper to taste, optional
chopped tomato or red bell pepper for garnish, optional

Chop bacon, fry until crisp and drain on paper towels. In a bowl, stir bacon into yogurt cheese and green onions. Taste and adjust seasonings. Sprinkle with tomato or red pepper if desired.

per tablespoon *24 calories, 2 g protein, 2 g carbo, 1 g fat, 48 mg sodium, 37% calories from fat*

112   SPREADS, DIPS AND SAUCES

AMARETTO CREAM

Serve this as a dip with a platter of fruit or pipe onto slices of fruit. Another possibility is to slit fruit down the center and pipe this mixture into the slit.

1 cup nonfat yogurt cheese
¼ cup confectioners' sugar, or more to taste
1-2 tbs. amaretto liqueur, or more to taste
toasted slivered almonds as ingredient or for garnish, optional

In a bowl, gently mix together all ingredients with a spoon. Taste and add more sugar or liqueur, if desired. If using chopped almonds, sprinkle on top or stir into mixture for texture and additional flavor.

per tablespoon   *24 calories, 2 g protein, 2 g carbo, 1 g fat, 48 mg sodium, 37% calories from fat*

CHOCOLATE CREAM DIP

Makes: 2¾ cups

This can be served as a topping for cakes or desserts, or as a dip for fruits. This recipe can also be used as a filling in cakes or between cookies, or to cover bananas and roll in a light coating of chopped nuts.

2 cups nonfat yogurt cheese
¼ cup sugar
⅓ cup semisweet chocolate chips
2 tbs. nonfat evaporated milk, whole milk or cream
1 tsp. vanilla extract

In a bowl, mix yogurt cheese and sugar together. Melt chocolate chips and stir in evaporated milk. Add yogurt cheese mixture and vanilla and stir gently. Refrigerate mixture for several hours before serving.

per tablespoon *23 calories, 1.5 g protein, 3.5 g carbo, 0.5 g fat, 16 mg sodium, 19% calories from fat*

TROPICAL SPREAD

Makes: 2¾ cups

Spread this tropical mixture over nut breads, or add it to a fruit platter. Use it as a spread for a chicken sandwich. For variety, add finely chopped dried apricots.

2 cups nonfat yogurt cheese
½ cup apricot preserves, or to taste

⅔ cup toasted flaked coconut
lemon juice, optional

In a bowl, mix together all ingredients, taste and add more apricot preserves, if desired. If mixture is too sweet for your taste, add a little lemon juice.

per tablespoon *27 calories, 1 g protein, 5 g carbo, 0.5 g fat, 19 mg sodium, 13% calories from fat*

CREAMY CRANBERRY SPREAD

Makes: 2⅔ cups

Consider this as a spread on a turkey sandwich or to serve with cranberry orange bread.

2 cups nonfat yogurt cheese
½ cup whole berry cranberry sauce

2 tbs. orange juice
1 tsp. grated fresh orange peel (zest)

In a bowl, mix together all ingredients, taste and adjust seasonings. Keep refrigerated until ready to use. The mixture thickens as it chills.

per tablespoon *17 calories, 1 g protein, 3 g carbo, trace fat, 17 mg sodium, 2% calories from fat*

HORSERADISH SAUCE

Use this as topping for potatoes, other starchy vegetables and roasted meats.

1½ cups nonfat yogurt cheese
½ cup horseradish

¼ cup finely chopped green onions, or
2 tbs. chopped chives, optional
salt and pepper to taste

In a bowl, combine all ingredients, taste and adjust seasonings. Keep refrigerated until ready to use.

per tablespoon   17 calories, 2 g protein, 2.5 g carbo, trace fat, NA sodium, 3% calories from fat

DILL SAUCE

Dill Sauce is ideal for fish dishes — and it makes a good dressing for potato salad.

1 cup nonfat yogurt cheese
½ cup chopped dill pickle
2 green onions, finely minced
1 tsp. dried dill weed

¼ tsp. celery seeds
½ tsp. Worcestershire sauce
2 tsp. lemon juice

In a bowl, mix all ingredients together. Taste and adjust seasonings. Cover and refrigerate for several hours before serving to allow flavors to blend.

per tablespoon   13 calories, 1 g protein, 2 g carbo, trace fat, 153 mg sodium, 4% calories from fat

DESSERTS

NEW YORK CHEESECAKE

Servings: 10-12

This recipe makes a dense New York-style cheesecake that is served without a crust. Make sure that you use yogurt cheese that has drained for at least 8 hours so the proper texture can be obtained.

4 cups well-drained nonfat yogurt
　　cheese
2 cups sugar
6 egg whites, or 3 eggs

1 tbs. fresh lemon juice
1 tsp. grated fresh lemon peel (zest)
1 tsp. vanilla extract
3 tbs. sifted cake flour

Preheat oven to 325°. Spray the sides and bottom of a 2-quart soufflé dish with nonstick cooking spray. Whip yogurt cheese with sugar, egg whites, lemon juice, lemon peel, vanilla and cake flour; do not overbeat. Pour into prepared dish and set into a large pan of hot water. Bake for 1½ hours or until cake is browned and cracked. Turn off oven and leave cake in oven for 1 hour longer. Remove cheesecake from water bath and allow to cool in dish on a wire rack for 1 hour. Place serving platter over dish and invert. Chill until ready to serve.

per serving *326 calories, 14 g protein, 66 g carbo, 1.5 g fat, 266 mg sodium, 4% calories from fat*

CHOCOLATE LIQUEUR CHEESECAKE

It's hard to believe that this absolutely delicious creamy cheesecake is so low in fat. Experimenting with alternative liqueurs such as amaretto, crème de mènthe, Frangelico, raspberry, etc., will create delicious varieties.

12 chocolate wafers, crushed
5 cups nonfat yogurt cheese
2 cups sugar
¾ cup cocoa powder
½ cup flour
½ cup chocolate liqueur or liqueur of choice

2 tsp. vanilla extract
½ tsp. salt
4 egg whites, or 2 eggs
¼ cup semisweet chocolate, melted

Preheat oven to 300°. Spray a 9-inch springform pan with nonstick cooking spray. Sprinkle chocolate crumbs in the bottom of pan. With a mixer or food processor, mix all remaining ingredients together until just combined; do not overbeat. Pour batter over crumbs and bake for 1¼ hours or until a knife inserted in the center comes out clean. Cool completely, cover and refrigerate for at least 8 hours before serving.

per serving   *463 calories, 17 g protein, 82 g carbo, 7 g fat, 401 mg sodium, 13% calories from fat*

LEMON CHEESECAKE

Servings: 12

This is a denser variety of cheesecake with an unusual oatmeal crust and topping. For decoration, sprinkle the top with sliced almonds and maraschino cherries.

2 cups quick oats
1/4 cup butter, melted
1/3 cup sugar
1 tbs. grated fresh lemon peel (zest)
1 tsp. cinnamon
6 egg whites, or 3 eggs
1 cup sugar
2/3 cup nonfat evaporated milk
2 tbs. flour
1/4 tsp. salt
2 tbs. lemon juice
2 tbs. grated fresh lemon peel (zest)
3 cups nonfat yogurt cheese

Preheat oven to 350°. Spray a 9-inch springform pan with nonstick cooking spray. In a bowl, mix together oats, butter, 1/3 cup sugar, 1 tbs. lemon peel and cinnamon. Press 1/2 of the mixture in the bottom of pan. With a mixer, beat egg whites or eggs well. Add sugar, evaporated milk, flour, salt, lemon juice and lemon peel and mix well. Add yogurt cheese and blend until just barely mixed.

Pour batter over crust and sprinkle with remaining oat mixture. Bake for 55 minutes or until a knife inserted in the center comes out clean. Remove from oven, cool to room temperature on a rack and refrigerate for several hours before serving.

per serving *259 calories, 14 g protein, 42 g carbo, 5 g fat, 203 mg sodium, 17% calories from fat*

STRAWBERRY ALMOND CHEESECAKE

Almond extract is substituted for the higher fat content of nuts, making this a low-fat version. Fresh strawberries make this a refreshing, light dessert.

½ cup vanilla wafer cookie crumbs
½ tsp. almond extract
3 cups (24 oz.) low-fat cottage cheese
2 cups nonfat yogurt cheese
¾ cup sugar
2 tbs. almond extract
2 eggs
4 egg whites
¼ tsp. cream of tartar
¼ cup sugar
2½ cups hulled strawberries
2 tbs. sugar, or to taste

Preheat oven to 325°. Spray a 9-inch springform pan with nonstick cooking spray. Mix vanilla wafer crumbs with 1/2 tsp. almond extract and sprinkle pan with crumbs. With a food processor or blender, process cottage cheese until smooth. Add yogurt cheese, 3/4 cup sugar, 2 tbs. almond extract and whole eggs and just barely process until smooth; do not overbeat. Beat egg whites with cream of tartar until soft peaks form. Gradually add 1/4 cup sugar and beat until stiff peaks form. Gently fold egg white mixture into cheese mixture. Pour into prepared pan and bake for 50 minutes. Cool to room temperature and refrigerate for at least 8 hours.

Slice or coarsely chop strawberries and combine with 2 tbs. sugar, or more to taste. Spread strawberries over top of cheesecake or serve on the side as a sauce.

per serving   *204 calories, 15 g protein, 31 g carbo, 2.5 g fat, 323 mg sodium, 11% calories from fat*

CHOCOLATE SWIRL CHEESECAKE

Servings: 12

A sprinkling of chocolate crust is perfect with this light vanilla and chocolate taste sensation. If you desire, serve in a "puddle" of chocolate or raspberry sauce.

¼ cup chocolate wafer cookie crumbs
24 oz. (3 cups) low-fat cottage cheese
1 cup sugar
4 egg whites, or 2 eggs
1 tsp. vanilla extract
2 cups nonfat yogurt cheese
3 tbs. cocoa powder
¼ cup sugar
4 egg whites
¼ tsp. cream of tartar

Preheat oven to 325°. Spray a 10-inch springform pan with nonstick cooking spray. Sprinkle cookie crumbs in pan. With a food processor or blender, blend together cottage cheese and 1 cup sugar until smooth. Add egg whites and vanilla and beat until smooth. Add yogurt cheese and blend until just mixed; do not overbeat. Place 3 cups of the cheese mixture into a separate bowl, add cocoa and 2 tbs. of the sugar and mix until just combined.

With a mixer, beat 4 egg whites with cream of tartar until soft peaks form. Add remaining sugar and beat until stiff peaks form. Fold ¼ of the beaten egg whites into cocoa mixture. Fold remaining egg whites into white cheese mixture. Pour white cheese mixture into springform pan. Gently spoon on chocolate mixture. With a knife, swirl chocolate through batter to create a marbleized effect. Bake for 50 minutes. Cool cake for at least 15 minutes at room temperature. Refrigerate for 8 hours before serving.

per serving *206 calories, 15 g protein, 32 g carbo, 2.5 g fat, 349 mg sodium, 10% calories from fat*

FROZEN MOCHA CHEESECAKE

This no-bake cheesecake can be whipped together in minutes. This should be made ahead of time and frozen for at least 6 hours before serving. For garnish, make rosettes with whipped topping and decorate with chocolate sprinkles or chocolate-covered coffee beans. Nonfat whipped topping is surprisingly good, but can't stand much handling.

1½ cups chocolate wafer cookie crumbs
2 tbs. sugar
1 can (14 oz.) nonfat sweetened
    condensed milk
¾ cup canned nonfat fudge topping

2 tbs. instant coffee powder
1 tsp. hot water
1 cup nonfat yogurt cheese
1 cup nonfat or low-fat whipped topping

In a small bowl, combine chocolate crumbs and sugar. Press mixture in the bottom of a 9-inch springform pan and chill in the freezer until the filling is made. With a mixer, beat together condensed milk and fudge topping. Mix instant coffee with hot water, add to fudge mixture and beat well. Add yogurt cheese and just barely mix to combine. Fold in whipped topping and pour into springform pan. Freeze for at least 6 hours before serving.

per serving *418 calories, 8 g protein, 89 g carbo, 11 g fat, 269 mg sodium, 20% calories from fat*

PINEAPPLE FROZEN YOGURT

Yogurt cheese makes a very creamy frozen yogurt. The advantage of using yogurt cheese over plain yogurt is that you can add undrained canned fruit, so the flavor of the fruit is intensified.

4 cups nonfat yogurt cheese
1 can (14 oz.) crushed pineapple with juice
1½ cups sugar, or more to taste

Mix all ingredients together and place in an ice cream maker. Freeze according to manufacturer's instructions, about 18 to 20 minutes on high speed, or until smooth and thick.

NOTE: If desired, toasted nuts can be added in the last few minutes of mixing.

per serving *200 calories, 9 g protein, 42 g carbo, 0.5 g fat, 116 mg sodium, 1% calories from fat*

RASPBERRY FROZEN YOGURT

Raspberries are my favorite berry and make a scrumptious light dessert after a heavy meal. For variety, add chopped chocolate pieces, toasted nuts or even a swirl of raspberry jam just before finishing the freezing process.

1¼ cups fresh or frozen raspberries
1-1½ cups sugar
4 cups nonfat yogurt cheese
few drops red food coloring, optional

Mix raspberries and 1 cup sugar together, breaking berries into small chunks. Mix sweetened berries with yogurt. Taste and add more sugar if necessary; add food coloring, if using. Freeze according to manufacturer's instructions for your ice cream maker, about 20 minutes. Remove from freezer unit and keep frozen until ready to serve.

per serving *154 calories, 9 g protein, 30 g carbo, 0.5 g fat, 116 mg sodium, 2% calories from fat*

STRAWBERRY BANANA YOGURT CREAM

Servings: 8

This simple dessert is full of good health, and makes a refreshing finale to a hearty meal.

2 cups mashed strawberries
2 bananas
1 cup nonfat yogurt cheese
sugar to taste, optional

Freeze mashed strawberries. Mash bananas and freeze. With a food processor or blender, mix together strawberries, bananas and yogurt cheese until blended. Taste and sweeten if desired. Serve immediately or freeze until ready to serve.

per serving   *74 calories, 4 g protein, 15 g carbo, 0.5 g fat, 44 mg sodium, 5% calories from fat*

CREAMY STRAWBERRY PIZZA

This recipe makes a quick, simple, light summer dessert. You can also use fresh raspberries and fresh blueberries. If you use yogurt cheese in place of butter for the crust, the results will be a slightly chewy crust as opposed to a flaky buttery crust.

1 cup nonfat yogurt cheese or butter
½ cup confectioners' sugar
1 cup flour
1 cup nonfat yogurt cheese
¾ cup confectioners' sugar

½ tsp. vanilla extract
1 qt. strawberries, hulled and sliced
1 cup bottled strawberry glaze
1 cup nonfat whipped topping, or low-fat

Preheat oven to 350°. Spray a 9-x-13-inch pan with nonstick cooking spray. In a bowl, mix 1 cup yogurt cheese, ½ cup confectioners' sugar and flour. Press mixture into prepared pan and bake for 15 minutes or until crust is lightly brown. Remove from oven and cool. Gently mix together 1 cup yogurt cheese, ¾ cup confectioners' sugar and vanilla. Spread mixture over cooled crust and top with sliced strawberries. Brush berries with strawberry glaze. Serve with a large dollop of whipped topping.

per serving *318 calories, 8 g protein, 96 g carbo, 0.5 g fat, 103 mg sodium, 1% calories from fat*

YOGURT FLAN

Yogurt adds a slight tang to the flan as well as a slightly denser texture. The nuts and whipped topping garnish are optional.

½ cup sugar
1 can (14 oz.) nonfat sweetened
   condensed milk
1 can (13 oz.) nonfat evaporated milk
3 eggs

1 tsp. vanilla extract
¾ cup nonfat yogurt cheese
whipped topping for garnish, optional
toasted chopped almonds for garnish,
   optional

Preheat oven to 350°. Heat sugar in a heavy saucepan over low heat until sugar just begins to turn brown (stir to help sugar caramelize evenly). Immediately pour caramelized sugar into a 9-inch glass pie dish and spread evenly. With a mixer, beat condensed milk, evaporated milk, eggs and vanilla together. Quickly beat in yogurt cheese; do not overbeat. Pour into pie dish and set dish in a larger pan. Pour warm water into large dish until water is within ½-inch of pie dish lip. Bake in 350° oven for 50 to 60 minutes or until a knife inserted in the center comes out clean. Cool before inverting onto a serving plate. Garnish with whipped topping and toasted almonds, if using.

per serving *184 calories, 7 g protein, 35 g carbo, 1.5 g fat, 83 mg sodium, 8% calories from fat*

CHERRY TEA CAKE

This delicious cake is flavored with cherry and orange. It can be sliced and served plain or with Cherry Yogurt Cream.

2½ cups flour
2 tsp. baking powder
½ tsp. soda
½ tsp. salt
1 tsp. cinnamon
¼ tsp. allspice
¼ cup applesauce or softened butter
1 cup brown sugar, packed
2 egg whites, or 1 large egg
1 cup chopped, pitted dark sweet cherries
¾ cup nonfat plain, cherry or orange yogurt cheese
¼ cup orange juice
1 tbs. grated fresh orange peel (zest)
¾ cup chopped walnuts, optional
confectioners' sugar, optional

Preheat oven to 350°. Cut brown paper to fit the bottom of a loaf pan and spray paper and sides with nonstick cooking spray. Sift together flour, baking powder, soda, salt, cinnamon and allspice. In a bowl, mix applesauce and brown sugar together and beat in egg whites. Stir in cherries, yogurt cheese, orange juice and orange peel. Add flour mixture, a little at a time, and stir until just mixed. Stir in nuts, if using. Pour mixture into prepared loaf pan and bake for 45 to 50 minutes or until a knife inserted in the center comes out clean. Remove from oven, cool for 5 minutes and remove from pan. If desired, dust with confectioners' sugar.

per serving   192 calories, 5 g protein, 42 g carbo, 0.5 g fat, 208 mg sodium, 2% calories from fat

CHERRY YOGURT CREAM
Makes: 2 cups

1 cup nonfat plain, cherry or orange yogurt cheese
2/3 cup light brown sugar, packed
1 tbs. lemon juice
1/2 cup chopped, pitted dark sweet cherries

In a bowl, stir yogurt cheese, brown sugar and lemon juice together. Stir in cherries. Serve in a bowl beside cake.

per tablespoon   19 calories, 1 g protein, 4 g carbo, trace fat, 12 mg sodium, 3% calories from fat

POPPY SEED CAKE

Yogurt cheese makes this a moist cake, and a tinge of orange tantalizes the taste buds. If you're watching fat intake and use applesauce instead of butter, you can have your cake and eat it too!

⅓ cup nonfat milk
¾ cup poppy seeds
¾ cup applesauce or softened butter
1½ cups sugar
8 egg whites
1 cup nonfat yogurt cheese
1½ tsp. vanilla or orange extract
1 tbs. grated fresh orange peel (zest)
2½ cups flour
1 tsp. baking soda
1 tsp. salt
sifted confectioners' sugar for garnish

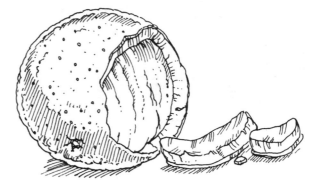

Preheat oven to 325°. Spray a 10-inch Bundt pan with nonstick cooking spray and coat with flour. Heat milk in a saucepan and add poppy seeds. Remove from heat and set aside for 2 hours to allow poppy seeds to absorb milk. In a bowl, mix applesauce and sugar together. Add 4 of the egg whites, mixing well. Stir in yogurt cheese, vanilla extract and orange peel. Sift together flour, soda and salt. Add flour mixture to applesauce mixture and stir until just barely combined.

Beat remaining 4 egg whites until stiff peaks form. Carefully fold egg whites and poppy seed mixture into applesauce mixture. Spoon batter into prepared Bundt pan and bake for 1 hour or until a knife inserted in the cake comes out clean. Remove from oven and cool on a rack for 10 minutes before inverting onto a plate. When cake is cooled, sprinkle with confectioners' sugar.

per serving *272 calories, 9 g protein, 50 g carbo, 4 g fat, 140 mg sodium, 14% calories from fat*

FRUITED EASTER CAKE

This rich cake is loaded with fruits and nuts. It needs no icing — just sprinkle with a little confectioners' sugar. The nuts add 4 grams of fat per serving. You can, as always, reduce the amount of nuts to reduce the fat.

⅔ cup chopped pecans
½ cup coarsely chopped candied cherries
½ cup coarsely chopped candied pineapple
1 tbs. flour
3 tbs. sugar
½ tsp. cinnamon
¾ cup applesauce or softened butter
1½ cups sugar
6 egg whites, or 3 eggs
2 tsp. vanilla extract
3 cups flour
1½ tsp. baking soda
1½ tsp. baking powder
1 tsp. salt
1½ cups nonfat yogurt cheese
2 tbs. sifted confectioners' sugar for garnish

Preheat oven to 350°. Spray a 10-inch Bundt pan with nonstick cooking spray and coat with flour. In a small bowl, combine pecans, candied cherries, candied pineapple and 1 tbs. flour; set aside. Mix 3 tbs. sugar and cinnamon and set aside. In a bowl, mix applesauce and sugar together until fluffy. Beat in egg whites and vanilla. Sift together flour, baking soda, baking powder and salt. Add dry ingredients to applesauce mixture alternately with yogurt cheese, beginning and ending with dry ingredients, and stirring to just barely combine.

Spoon $\frac{1}{2}$ of the batter into prepared Bundt pan, spoon on nut and fruit mixture, sprinkle with cinnamon sugar mixture and cover with remaining batter. Bake for 1 hour or until a knife inserted in the center comes out clean. Remove from oven and cool for 15 minutes before inverting onto a plate. When cool, sift confectioners' sugar on top of cake for decoration.

per serving *383 calories, 9 g protein, 78 g carbo, 4.5 g fat, 408 mg sodium, 10% calories from fat*

PECAN COFFEECAKE

Yogurt cheese makes this cake moist and is ideal served for breakfast or as a dessert. It's good served warm with a dollop of whipped topping or yogurt.

1/2 cup applesauce or softened butter
1 cup sugar
6 egg whites, or 3 eggs
2 cups sifted flour
1 tsp. baking powder
1 tsp. baking soda
1/4 tsp. salt
1 cup nonfat yogurt cheese
3/4 cup golden raisins
3/4 cup brown sugar, packed
1 tbs. flour
1 1/2 tsp. cinnamon
2 tbs. butter
1 1/4 cups chopped pecans

Preheat oven to 350°. Spray a 9-x-13-inch pan with nonstick cooking spray. In a bowl, mix applesauce and sugar together until fluffy. Add egg whites and beat well. Sift 2 cups flour, baking powder, baking soda and salt together. Add dry ingredients to applesauce mixture alternately with yogurt cheese, stirring to just barely combine. Stir in raisins. Pour into prepared pan. In a small bowl, mix together brown sugar, 1 tbs. flour and cinnamon. Cut in butter until it resembles cornmeal and stir in pecans. Sprinkle this mixture on top of batter. Bake for 30 minutes or until knife inserted in the center comes out clean.

per serving 359 calories, 7 g protein, 60 g carbo, 11 g fat, 219 mg sodium, 28% calories from fat

APPLE YOGURT CAKE

Adding yogurt to this recipe results in a delicious moist cake studded with apples and flavored with cinnamon.

1½ cups sifted flour
½ cup sugar
2 tsp. baking powder
½ tsp. salt
½ tsp. cinnamon
½ cup nonfat milk

¼ cup butter or applesauce
4 egg whites, or 2 eggs
1 cup diced peeled apples
½ cup nonfat yogurt cheese
⅓ cup sugar
½ cup chopped walnuts, optional

Preheat oven to 375°. Spray an 8-inch baking pan with nonstick cooking spray. In a bowl, mix together flour, sugar, baking powder, salt and cinnamon. Add milk, butter and 2 egg whites or 1 egg; stir until just mixed. Stir in apples and pour into prepared pan. In a separate bowl, beat remaining egg whites or egg and yogurt cheese until just blended and spread mixture over cake batter. Mix together sugar and walnuts, if using, and sprinkle over yogurt mixture. Bake for 30 minutes or until a knife inserted in the center comes out clean.

per serving *224 calories, 6 g protein, 39 g carbo, 5 g fat, 287 mg sodium, 21% calories from fat*

CREAMY RHUBARB PIE

You'll love this delicious creamy version of an old-time favorite. For an even a better treat, toast the almonds before garnishing the pie. For a change, use the oat-almond crust from the pumpkin pie recipe, page 142.

4 cups rhubarb, cut into 1-inch pieces
2½ cups sugar, or more to taste
3 tbs. cornstarch
¼ tsp. salt
one 9-inch unbaked pie crust

1 cup nonfat yogurt cheese
4 egg whites, or 2 eggs, beaten
1 cup nonfat sour cream
½ cup sliced almonds for garnish

Preheat oven to 425°. In a 2-quart saucepan, cook rhubarb, 2 cups of the sugar, cornstarch and salt together over medium heat until mixture boils and thickens, stirring constantly. Pour rhubarb mixture into pie crust and bake for 15 minutes. Meanwhile, in a small bowl, mix together yogurt cheese, egg whites, and remaining ½ cup sugar using a spoon; do not overbeat. Pour mixture over partially baked pie. Reduce oven temperature to 350°. Bake for 25 minutes or until topping is set. Cool on a rack to room temperature. Spoon sour cream on top and refrigerate for several hours before serving. Just before serving, sprinkle with sliced almonds.

per serving *487 calories, 37 g protein, 152 g carbo, 11 g fat, 237 mg sodium, 11% calories from fat*

PUMPKIN PIE WITH OAT CRUST

Servings: 8

If you are looking for a healthier version of pumpkin pie, look no further. The crust will be a little crumbly but has a nice nutty flavor.

1¼ cups oats
1½ cups almonds
2-3 tbs. sugar, brown sugar or date sugar
½ tsp. salt
4-5 tbs. nonfat milk
2 cups canned pumpkin
1 cup sugar
1 tsp. vanilla extract
1 egg
½ tsp. salt
1 tsp. cinnamon
½ tsp. ginger
¼ tsp. nutmeg
pinch ground cloves
2 cups nonfat yogurt cheese

Preheat oven to 350 °. Place oats and almonds in a food processor or blender container and process until finely ground. Add sugar, salt and enough milk to hold mixture together (mixture will be a little crumbly). Roll dough between 2 pieces of waxed paper and line a 10-inch pie plate. Place remaining ingredients, except yogurt cheese, in a bowl and whisk ingredients together until well blended. Whisk in yogurt cheese and pour into pie crust. Bake for 1 hour and 15 minutes.

per serving   *419 calories, 16 g protein, 58 g carbo, 16 g fat, 372 mg sodium, 33% calories from fat*

PUMPKIN CHEESE ROLL

A reduced-fat filling makes this family favorite even more appealing. If you use nuts, toasting them adds a lot more flavor and in a refrigerated dessert helps keep the nuts from turning soft. Reduce or eliminate nuts for a lighter dessert.

1½ cups chopped walnuts, optional
6 egg whites, or 3 eggs
1 cup sugar
⅔ cup canned pumpkin
1 tsp. lemon juice
¾ cup flour
1 tsp. baking powder
2 tsp. cinnamon
1 tsp. ginger
½ tsp. nutmeg
½ tsp. salt
2 tbs. confectioners' sugar
1¼ cups nonfat yogurt cheese
1 cup confectioners' sugar, sifted
½ tsp. vanilla extract
confectioners' sugar for garnish, optional

Preheat oven to 375°. Spray a 10-x-15-inch jelly roll pan with nonstick cooking spray and sprinkle with flour. If you use walnuts, place them on a baking sheet and partially toast in oven for about 8 minutes and set aside to cool. With a mixer, beat egg whites for 5 minutes at high speed. Gradually add sugar. Beat in pumpkin and lemon juice. Mix together flour, baking powder, cinnamon, ginger, nutmeg and salt; fold gently into egg mixture. Pour batter into prepared pan. Sprinkle lightly toasted nuts on top, if using. Bake for 10 to 15 minutes or until a light touch does not leave a finger mark. Sprinkle confectioners' sugar on a flat-weave dishtowel. Remove pan from oven and run a knife around the edge. Quickly invert pan onto sugared towel and immediately roll up from the short edge. Cool cake completely before filling.

In a bowl, gently mix together yogurt cheese, confectioners' sugar and vanilla. Do not beat in a mixer. Very gently unroll cake and spread with filling. Roll back up and chill in refrigerator until ready to serve. If desired, sprinkle with confectioners' sugar for garnish.

per serving *199 calories, 6 g protein, 44 g carbo, trace fat, 106 mg sodium, 1% calories from fat*

BANANA NUT COOKIES

These cookies are a healthy sweet treat that can be varied by using different types of flour or mixing the types of nuts.

1½ cups flour
1 tsp. salt
3 cups rolled oats
½ cup sugar
6 bananas, mashed
1 cup nonfat yogurt cheese
2 tsp. vanilla extract
1 cup chopped toasted nuts

Preheat oven to 325°. In a bowl, mix flour, salt, oats and sugar together. Gently stir in bananas, yogurt cheese, vanilla and nuts. Drop by spoonfuls onto a baking sheet sprayed with nonstick cooking spray. Bake for about 12 to 15 minutes or until light brown.

per serving *100 calories, 3 g protein, 17 g carbo, 2.5 g fat, 70 mg sodium, 23% calories from fat*

GRAPES AND CREAM

Servings: 6

A light dessert is ideal after a heavy meal, and this one is quick to fix. Remember that yogurt cheese should never be over-processed because it tends to thin the texture down too much.

2 tbs. grated fresh orange peel (zest)
¾ cup brown sugar, packed
2 tbs. orange juice
1 cup nonfat yogurt cheese
1 lb. seedless green grapes

In a bowl, mix together orange peel, brown sugar, orange juice and yogurt cheese until just barely mixed. Pour mixture over grapes and chill until ready to serve.

per serving *202 calories, 5 g protein, 47 g carbo, 0.5 g fat, 68 mg sodium, 3% calories from fat*

LEMON CREAM WITH BLUEBERRY SAUCE

Servings: 8

This light, creamy, chilled dessert is topped with blueberry sauce. For a little crunch, sprinkle with chopped toasted nuts, granola or graham cracker crumbs.

1 cup nonfat milk
2 tsp. coriander seeds, crushed
1 tbs. grated fresh lemon peel (zest)
2 egg yolks
1 cup sugar
2 pkg. (1/4 oz. each) unflavored gelatin
1/2 cup cold water
1/4 tsp. salt
4 cups nonfat yogurt cheese
1/2 cup lemon juice
1 tsp. vanilla extract
1 1/2 cups frozen blueberries, thawed
2-3 tbs. sugar
pinch mace or nutmeg
pinch salt
1 tsp. cornstarch
1 tbs. water

Place milk, coriander seeds and lemon peel in a heavy saucepan, bring to a boil, remove from heat, cover and steep for 20 minutes. Strain steeped milk, and whisk in egg yolks and 1 cup sugar. Mix gelatin with cold water and stir into milk mixture with 1/4 tsp. salt. Cook over medium heat, stirring constantly until mixture thickens, about 5 minutes. Remove from heat and set aside.

In a bowl, combine yogurt cheese, lemon juice and vanilla extract. Fold yogurt mixture into cooled milk mixture, pour into parfait glasses or wine glasses and chill for several hours.

In a heavy saucepan, place blueberries, 2 tsp. sugar, mace and salt; stir to combine. Mix cornstarch with water and add to blueberry mixture. Cook over medium heat, stirring constantly until mixture thickens. Remove from heat and cool to room temperature. Spoon blueberry sauce on top of lemon cream and serve.

per serving   *286 calories, 17 g protein, 53 g carbo, 2 g fat, 293 mg sodium, 6% calories from fat*

INDEX

SERVE CREATIVE, EASY, NUTRITIOUS MEALS WITH nitty gritty® COOKBOOKS

Entrées From Your Bread Machine
Muffins, Nut Breads and More
Healthy Snacks for Kids
100 Dynamite Desserts
Recipes for Yogurt Cheese
Sautés
Cooking in Porcelain
Appetizers
Recipes for the Loaf Pan
Casseroles
The Best Bagels are made at home*
   (*perfect for your bread machine)
The Toaster Oven Cookbook
Skewer Cooking on the Grill
Creative Mexican Cooking
Extra-Special Crockery Pot Recipes
Cooking in Clay
Marinades
Deep Fried Indulgences
Cooking with Parchment Paper
The Garlic Cookbook
Flatbreads From Around the World
From Your Ice Cream Maker

Favorite Cookie Recipes
Cappuccino/Espresso: The Book of
   Beverages
Indoor Grilling
Slow Cooking
The Best Pizza is made at home*
   (*perfect for your bread machine)
The Well Dressed Potato
Convection Oven Cookery
The Steamer Cookbook
The Pasta Machine Cookbook
The Versatile Rice Cooker
The Dehydrator Cookbook
The Bread Machine Cookbook
The Bread Machine Cookbook II
The Bread Machine Cookbook III
The Bread Machine Cookbook IV:
   Whole Grains and Natural Sugars
The Bread Machine Cookbook V:
   Favorite Recipes from 100 Kitchens
The Bread Machine Cookbook VI:
   *Hand-Shaped Breads from the
   Dough Cycle*

Worldwide Sourdoughs From Your
   Bread Machine
Recipes for the Pressure Cooker
The New Blender Book
The Sandwich Maker Cookbook
Waffles
The Coffee Book
The Juicer Book
The Juicer Book II
Bread Baking (traditional)
No Salt, No Sugar, No Fat Cookbook
Cooking for 1 or 2
Quick and Easy Pasta Recipes
The 9x13 Pan Cookbook
Low Fat American Favorites
Now That's Italian!
Low Salt, Low Sugar, Low Fat Desserts
Healthy Cooking on the Run
The Wok
Favorite Seafood Recipes
New International Fondue Cookbook

For a free catalog, write or call:
Bristol Publishing Enterprises, Inc.
P.O. Box 1737
San Leandro, CA 94577